Heal

You Have the Power

Powerful Stories of Healing
Providing Hope and Inspiration

Volume 2

ISBN: #9798633001020

Compiled by: DeeAnne Riendeau

Edited by: Ashara Love, Darlene Blischack and Theresa Franson

Published by: Your Holistic Earth

Cover design & layout by: Darlene Mitansky, Wingspan Studio www.wingspanstudio.com

Visit Your Holistic Earth at www.yourholisticearth.ca

Contents

Preface
YOU Have the Power to HEAL!
By DeeAnne Riendeau

As I write this, the world is facing an unprecedented challenge. A virus called Covid-19 has taken its grip upon humankind and we are in a pandemic. Schools have been closed; nonessential service providers have been asked to close business. We have been asked to shelter in place and practice social distancing. Our world has changed almost overnight. Fear and anxiety have risen to the surface and now more than ever before, creating hope and nurturing connection is of the most vital importance.

This book is a direct response to the health crisis we have been facing for years and now it is becoming even more vital. This compilation of healing stories is meant to inspire, to give hope, and to remind humankind that each one of us has the power to truly heal ourselves.

For a decade now, I have been speaking about an existing health crisis. However, until now, many didn't want to hear what I had to say. When doing presentations, I would say the "zombie" apocalypse was already here and we were the zombies walking around hooked to our phones, hooked on coffee, drugs, booze, food, whatever we could to fill the "voids." We have become an addicted society, lost in the day to day "busy"ness, not able to be truly present. Chronic illness has been increasing at alarming rates. Mental illness is taking more lives than ever before. And until two weeks ago, nothing was changing, nothing significantly at least. For the most part, we all just kept going and ignoring that we were spiraling downward quickly. We had gotten so far away from ourselves that we could not hear our bodies, minds, and spirits calling us home.

We can no longer ignore it. In the last few weeks, restrictions on travel and requirements for self-isolation and quarantines has started to create a wide and deep worldly shift.

Here is the perspective I invite you to explore. What if Covid-19 is the cure for all that was wrong with the world? What if this virus helps us to see that the way we were doing things was the problem? What if we were lost and this virus will bring us "home" again?

The virus has caused everyone to slow down. It has caused everyone to reflect on what was. You see, there is an invitation for us to truly change how we were doing things and re-evaluate our lives. This is a catalyst and I will admit, it is intense, and it is not easy right now. This much change, this quickly, has us all a bit rattled and feelings of uncertainty are in our faces daily. These changes have been devastating to some. Loss of work, complete isolation, kids no longer in schools, limits on daycare just to name

4

a few. The economic toll this will have is yet to be seen and felt fully. We do not know what will happen or how long this will last. However, we will get through this. We will work together; we will dig in and we will come out of this better than ever before. I believe this fully without a doubt and already I see a growing number of beautiful stories coming from this.

The connection we have with ourselves is getting stronger and the connection between loved ones is becoming deeper. Families are spending time together playing games and getting creative. We hear stories of people singing from balconies and loved ones helping gather groceries and necessary items for those in isolation. So much goodness!

Even more so the impact this is having on the earth itself has been profound. Pollution has gone down because nobody is travelling and going out. Dolphins swim the canals in Italy once again. Powerful positive change on a worldwide spectrum has already shown itself!

If we want to truly change our lives it is time for each and every one of us to stand in our power. To listen to the truth of what is being shown to us. This book is to help us see that we have the power within us. We have had it all along. The power to be better, stronger, healthier with each moment that passes.

Let these stories be your medicine. Let them inspire and show you the possibilities. These stories cover mental, physical, spiritual, and financial health and take you to all aspects of yourself. I invite you to let them speak to you and ignite the spark within you for greatness.

We are always looking for co-authors who have stories to share. Please inquire at info@yourholisticearth.ca

5

Foreword
By Corey Poirier

Now, more than ever, this book is desperately needed. As I write this, people are in the midst of widespread panic over a new virus called Coronavirus/COVID-19. People are stockpiling toilet paper at a more rapid pace than food (to the amazement of others). Some are saying it will change the world as we know it, others are glued to the news, and others are saying it's basically the next SARS, West Nile Virus, or Zika.

That is, those people are saying it is to be taken seriously, but more from a precautionary perspective: not to be viewed as the end of civilization or a reason to act irrationally, and certainly not a reason to build a bunker and check out of civilization for the next twenty years.

In moments like this, precautions are wise, and one death is too many, but today SARS, West Nile, and Zika are all just a distant memory, and something very few give any thought to. But at the time... many people were in quite an uproar.

What's perhaps perplexing is that people ignore the fact that we are taking bigger risks every time we walk out the door each day than we are living without fear during times like these.

I mean just look at the numbers around car accident deaths each year. Yet, imagine if we simply chose to stay home every day because there is an assumed risk involved in "living life" each day – I want to ask you: what kind of life would that really be?

I mentioned the Coronavirus above as if I'm introducing it to some people even though pretty much everyone has all but heard of it as of this writing. I see this book as being timeless, and once things are back to "normal," if you're reading this years later, it may not seem as current as it does to me writing this, so I thought I should introduce it as if you might not have heard of it.

Now, while the news is reporting all the numbers and the reasons you should be afraid, the one thing the news is not reporting is the impact the widespread panic, and yes, fear mongering, has on people's minds and bodies.

Is it possible that the fear itself can make you more susceptible to viruses like these in the first place? Is it possible that fear can weaken your immune system and increase your chances of falling ill?

I think most of us, and certainly you who are reading this book, know it's more than possible, it has been proven.

So again, I say yes, it's important to take precautions. For instance, yes, strengthen your immune system, sneeze into your sleeves rather than on your hands, wash your hands and don't touch your face after touching doors and walls in public places.

However these are things you should be doing anyway. What I'm also saying though is this: don't worry yourself sick.

My main concern right now is about the impact, as mentioned, this energy is having on people as a whole. People are far from at-ease right now, and that is exactly what creates dis-ease later.

As a recovering Hypochondriac myself, I know first-hand the impact this whole ordeal will have on people, inside and out.

That is exactly why I think we need, yes, another book on the power of HEALING.

It is my hope that within these pages, through the stories of the authors who are sharing their message so freely, you find clues, road signs, and secrets to healing that which ails you – even if it is fears over what awaits you each day on your journey.

The answer will be different for everyone, which is the power of having so many contributors involved in this type of project.

For me, when I first began battling Hypochondria, it was after a two-year battle with generalized anxiety. I was having balance problems, concentration problems, I was paranoid over almost everything, and I was consumed by negative thoughts.

When I discovered yoga, meditation, holistic healing, and finally, my calling in life – I ultimately discovered the tools I needed to HEAL myself, with the help of others of course.

My life has been the better for it every day since.

What your answer is, I do not know, but I am optimistic you will find something that sparks a bit of a light bulb/aha/EUREKA moment for you within the pages of HEAL.

If it doesn't for some reason, and you are on a search for wellness that requires more information and support, you are certainly in the right place, as the practitioners and staff of Your Holistic Earth and the non-for-profit division AIMHH, are here to assist you in finding the information you need to move your healing journey forward.

Until then, here's to your greater health.

Corey Poirier is a multiple-time TEDx, MoMondays, and PMx Speaker. He is the host of the top rated 'Let's Do Influencing' Show, the 'Get Paid To Speak' show, founder of The Speaking Program, bLU Talks, and featured in multiple television specials.

A columnist with Entrepreneur and Forbes magazine, he has been featured on CBS, CTV, NBC, ABC, is a Forbes Coaches Council member, and is one of the few leaders featured twice on the popular Entrepreneur on Fire show.

Corey has also interviewed over 5,000 of the world's top leaders.

A father to his young son Sebastian, boyfriend to Shelley and a father to 2 fur-babies, Corey is also a practicing Yogi and Rock Recording of the Year Nominee.

Corey Poirier
Email: thatspeakerguy@gmail.com | www.thatspeakerguy.com

Reflecting the Light of Love
By Amber Von Grat

When I was little, one of my biggest fears was being trapped alone in the dark, feeling helpless in a blind attempt to escape.

If you told 8-year-old me that my imagination could fool me, I still would have opted to embrace my failed understanding of love, rather than to have never loved at all. Perhaps the way that I suffered allowed me to see the suffering around me. Losing myself in the dark was admirable compared to the pain that came with finding the light.

He came to me with brown sugar skin and hands that moved my soul when they touched my skin. The scripted words I drew on his back got lost in the indents of his skin and burned a desire in my heart: a desire to love and be loved.

I might be lost in the first three letters of *remembering*, because I forget the last time I was a dreamer. And tonight I want to fall asleep.

I want to close my eyes and create stars in the darkness. I want to fuse my thoughts together with your memories, to create constellations that complement the work of arteries that mark your heart, so every time I think of you, our stars will shine brighter than the moon.

I want to let our hands collide and memorize every indent and crossroad in your fingerprints. I want all my senses to get lost and then find the sixth from the sparks of our souls setting fire in the presence of your palms.

I want to rest my head on your chest and give every vibration a beat to listen to. I want to tangle our feet and feel the soft layers of sheets underneath; surrounding our bodies and shaping us into one.

When I wake up, I'll find memories from today in a shooting star that will course the rivers that run through your heart and a bonfire, lit by a sixth sense, that will cause our souls to dance to a beating drum that will never forget your rhythm.

This is what I thought love was: expressive, romantic, creative, intricate, and intimate. I believed in setting my soul on fire with a burning passion that couldn't and shouldn't be tamed, when in reality, that kind of expression was a firepit of lust and anger fueled by the ashes of desire.

Maybe he dropped to his knees out of embarrassment. Maybe he cried the first time because he knew betrayal should hurt. Maybe I stayed because I felt he needed me. Maybe he still deserved my love. Maybe if I stayed, he would learn that the worst parts of him still deserved compassion and mercy. If the benefit of the doubt was unconditional love, then it isn't a question of why, it was a question of how.

It felt as though I had just gasped for a breath of fresh air, when the weight of his hello began to drown me again. The butterflies in my stomach chased goosebumps up my spine and hid under the wounded heart on my sleeve. My heart was consistently lashed with the tally of women he fed hope to. The irony of it all was that I was more than willing and he was less than capable.

I remember waking up to my whole world falling to pieces.

We were not alone.

My heart dropped to the pit of my stomach when I found out that he had betrayed me while his entire family and I were upstairs sleeping.

The childhood friend that I shouldn't worry about. The girl who couldn't make it to the birthday party. The neighbour. The one from the job interview. The one from milfaholics.com. The BBW. The 3 am call. The one from Calgary. The one from Twitter. The one with my name. The one from wrestling.

I should have believed him when he called himself a sociopath, but I was apparently the crazy one – so I went to a professional for confirmation.

It took searching on the university website page, free of cost and offering convenience, and most importantly, me wanting help, to get professional advice. The posters didn't do justice for my level of anxiety, but I pleaded guilty when I started to answer the questions for the first consultation.

Why are you here?

Great question. Something is wrong. I'm what is wrong. After all, I am the one here alone and no matter what I did, nothing was ever good enough.

Circle one. Anxiety. Depression. Relationship problems. Abuse.

There it is. Abuse. I'm a smart girl, I know what the definition of abuse is: cruelty with repetition. The intention was there too. The blackouts. The lies. The deception.

I immediately burst into tears when she said it out loud, and I admitted to being emotionally abused by my best friend and boyfriend for years.

So who am I?

I was asked what I want to be remembered for, when I'm gone.

I told him this.

When I'm gone, I want the world to know that no matter what I had done in my life, my biggest accomplishment was loving everyone and everything that I could, without hesitation or expectation and in need of no recognition.

When I'm gone, I want you to look at the round photo of me on the front of a booklet full of memories and see happiness in my smile. I want you to wonder where I'm looking and know that I found beauty in every circumstance.

When I'm gone, I want it known that I had my mother's strength and courage to be brave. Remember that I always fought for what I wanted, and I kept a smile even when the tears fought their way through from my deepest fears.

When I'm gone, I want you to see past my beauty and feel my soul still around you, holding you, and telling you everything will be ok.

When I'm gone, I want you to know that everything happens for a reason. That heartache and bruises only last as long as you let them. I want you to know that I made difficult choices and I have no regrets.

When I'm gone, I want you to understand that being naive isn't so bad. I may not have always fit in, but I never lost sight of who I was, and I know that my mind is what makes me different.

When I'm gone, I want you to know that with love comes vulnerability, but we can find peace in weaknesses as they disappear, when love perseveres.

I told her this:

First of all, I am a brown eyed girl to my father, whose only wish was to live to walk me down the aisle and to remind me that he loved me more than anything.

Secondly, I am the daughter of a mother who walked through hell to ensure I received the love everyone promised me but could never fully commit to.

Lastly, I am suffering from the reality that I am now responsible for another human being's understanding of love, and I am not convinced that I can prove that it exists.

For the first three weeks, everything made me sick. The next three, he soothed us to sleep by rubbing my belly and saying goodnight, only to make himself forget until morning.

There wasn't affection in the mornings. It was a scheduled reassurance before he went on with whomever he had planned to see that day. The mother and fiancée title felt like a mirage; I did not know how much longer the illusion would last. Maybe going to Ontario to meet his family to celebrate his birthday would change things.

He stayed there for two weeks, and I visited for one. I can still hear her voice complimenting my ring and sitting down beside me while we played board games with his friends in the living room.

She had slept with him the week before I got there. He had told her it wasn't an engagement ring. The persistence of his denials gnawed on my insides as I laid my judgment to bed and had faith regardless of his lies.

The night before we were to return to our home base, I cried myself to sleep, nauseous from the innocence in my stomach, ignoring the intuition in my chest, the whispers that were telling me we weren't going to make it.

My tears drowned out the sound of footsteps as a different female snuck into his parents' home to feed his ego before we headed home. All I can say is that I am thankful that I didn't go downstairs and that he got what he wanted when he wanted it.

It took 24 hours for my intuition to kick in. I opened his Apple Watch and I found hundreds of messages – proof of his infidelity. I wanted to throw up. His claims of innocence echoed: I had no right to be concerned just because he could handle friendships with other women.

It was all a lie. I wasn't important, wanted, or needed beyond what my body could offer, and even then, it still was not enough. It broke me.

I imagined my future as it stood starkly in front of me. I thought about my child growing up into a home where someone was pretending to be someone they were not. My anxiety skyrocketed, along with the nausea and heartache.

It took me awhile to figure it out, but like pieces to a puzzle, I soon got the picture clear in my mind.

You need to start on the outside and work your way in to see the whole picture. I picked the pieces out, all mixed up, not knowing where to begin. Hoping that one day, when I looked down at the puzzle, I could still make out a picture of me.

Suddenly, being alone and trapped in a dark empty room starts to feel more real than believing you can earn someone's love. As a little girl, you believe that everyone loves you. That your light will shine as far and as wide as your mother's hand took you. When you get older and start to explore the world looking for love, and you do not find it; it finds you.

Every part of yourself that is lacking, that you have yet to understand, is waiting to teach you a lesson: to look at your own reflection.

I cannot describe how it felt to be fooled into believing that someone loves you or how the love you imagined was nothing but an illusion. I cannot tell you how many times I was proven wrong when it came to believing that I was loved, but I can tell you that my dignity was sacrificed. I started to believe that I had nothing to offer except what people could take from me.

I learned a terrible lesson: My love was only worthless if I made it worthy, and it couldn't be stolen if there was nothing to steal.

Perhaps an even more devastating choice is equating contentment with happiness and believing that protection comes in the form of deception. Regardless, the biggest form of deception is when you continue to lie to yourself. Because losing yourself in the dark is nothing compared to the pain that comes when you step into the light of truth.

You are being dishonest with yourself by being attracted to something that isn't real: a point of view that has the best interest of itself instead of the benefit of one another. This creates false hope and results in your own downfall.

You become so absorbed in the past that you begin to be dishonest with yourself in the present. You compound the damage by valuing an assumption: convincing yourself that you're doing it for the benefit of the future, rather than accepting the truth, in order to survive in the present.

My mind was remoulded to what others believed to be true. Even when I spoke my truth out loud, their perspective still seemed to make more sense. It was easier to believe that I was wrong about everything and start over, than to believe that I was wrong about him.

My heart was shattered and I believed leading with my heart would only betray me again. I let the tears flow every night for months, wishing my dad was there to hold me and make me laugh. I couldn't tell my family because it would be a disappointment. They already knew I had done this to myself.

My body felt like an abandoned scapegoat for pain and anger. My vagina felt like a disposal site for a future he didn't need, the same future I'd always wanted. Some days felt like I could sit by a man. At other times, it felt like even holding someone's hand was only the beginning of a new illusion of what love was supposed to feel like.

My soul was abandoned. I began to believe that the truth of the world around me made more sense than the naive bubble I lived inside.

I started to hide from myself. I decided to become unrecognizable and disguise myself as the reflection of someone he would be with. Not because maybe he would want me again, but because deceiving myself protected me from feeling the pain that I would never wish on my worst enemy. I faced my fear with the truth of someone else's illusion, and I lost myself in the process.

Sex was for fun and pleasure.

Drugs were to escape pain and reality.

Money was for status and value.

Intimacy was for excitement and survival.

These beliefs were serving me, but they did not last long. Although it felt good to be in control of my definition of sex, drugs, money, and intimacy, the relationships I engaged in were empty. I chose to face my fear of betrayal with a willingness to be betrayed, because that expectation had more clarity.

The way I suffered allowed me to see the suffering around me; it became urgent for me to spend my life saving people experiencing emotional abuse and a corresponding attachment to the idea of love, rather than love itself.

Love, like most realities, transcends beyond what the eye can see. You can find love in the rustling of leaves on a cool fall morning, but you can only feel the invite of the wind as it twirls around you and asks you to dance.

I want you to know that you are who you are.

No one should judge you or cause you self doubt.

I want you to know that above all, your happiness is important.

You are human and you will make mistakes. How else will you learn?

Not everyone will see you as pleasing. Nobody can tell you who or what to love. You should never be afraid of taking control of your life. Be selfish and love yourself unconditionally. Never feel guilty for taking initiative. The strong will understand and the weak will only find comfort in manipulation.

The most beautiful thing about loving
a guarded girl isn't that she needs you.
She stopped needing people a long time ago.
It's because she wants you, and that's
the purest love of all.

Amber Von Grat is a Speaker, Soul Coach, and upcoming Author of *Soul Detox: 15 Principles to Discovering Your Truth and Freeing Your Spirit*, due in 2020.

As a Caucasian-Canadian female, Amber shares how her spiritual experience and relationship with God called her to Islam. A graduate of the University of Alberta Science of Kinesiology program, Amber was recruited as the first hijabi firefighter in Spruce Grove, Alberta. She resigned from fighting physical battles in the Fire Service Industry to pursue her passion for fighting the emotional, spiritual, and mental battles facing women of faith in the Muslim community.

Amber Von Grat
Phone: 780-886-9136 | Email: avongrat@ualberta.ca | Instagram: @ambervongrat

Resilience is Our Superpower

By Ashara Love

Today Is a New Day

The planetary 'system,' upon which all of life depends, is hurtling into a brick wall, according to scientists. It is reaching a point where crash, crumble, and correction are now clearly applied not just to the eco-collapse we are witnessing in its breathtaking speed, but to the unstable economy and the poorly funded and ill-maintained social structures we have relied on without DEMANDING real strength and deep foundation for far too long.

Starting a couple months ago, I began scribbling notes for the article I intended to write for this book. But hey, I was busy co-authoring and editing the other writers' magnificent tales. I knew I would end up writing mine after everyone else had submitted theirs.

I just couldn't connect. Nothing I wrote seemed relevant. It wasn't bad. It was my best effort, and I shall save what I wrote - the fragments of my thoughts - for another day, another blog, another project.

But today, inside a growing awareness of the massive shift we are experiencing right this minute, a thoughtbubble popped in my head as I stumbled towards my first cup of coffee, already brewed.

Resilience is Our Superpower

These words clarified what I really want to say, TODAY. I mean, whatever day it might be that you are reading my humble words, I'm certain the timing is perfect. I say hello from here. Wishing you well and healthy.

I am deeply and painfully aware that my silly little life is damn insignificant in the face of how fast we've been introduced to this immense wake-up call. It amazes me: the havoc a teeny-tiny invisible virus, affecting a very small percentage of humanity, can wreak upon our lives. Our NORMAL (which wasn't but we liked to tell ourselves that, didn't we?) is OVER. We cannot breathe a sigh of relief and go back to 'business as usual.'

If you are reading these words anywhere near today (March 17, 2020, the day I wrote this) perhaps you are still in shock. Maybe you, wise and wonderful and looking for answers, are asking: How did this even happen? So sudden!

Nope. Not really.

The predictions were consistent for decades. The scientists have been yelling. I listened, but didn't know what to do. That feeling of powerlessness permeated everything I tried to do with my psychedelic kaleidoscope of a life.

Economic cycles are reliable-every 12 years, the stock market craters. This is a known fact. Robert Kiyosaki told me so. The highly predictable crash cycles help the overly wealthy acquire MORE stock for cheap, while average investors lose everything. They follow a script that helps one another, while pretending they are following the rules the rest of us do. How is that working out?

I'm not here to derail the conversation around Healing. I am here to defend our right as human beings to access the options that work best for us: meaning that we have the RIGHT to choose the kind of health care that serves our best needs, rather than what our 'system' doles out like Scrooge on a bad day. That 'radical' stance certainly doesn't fit comfortably into the process we've had imposed upon us by people who DO. NOT. CARE.

That acquiescence absolutely impacts the situation we are watching, many helplessly, in this very moment. It DOESN'T have to be this way. It DOESN'T.

Why do we accept the crumbs of services and social structures that we pay dearly for in the first place? I am in awe of the blatant disregard for the well being of our citizens.

I hope that the shell game is well and truly over. The emperor's undies have been fully exposed. The System is vaporwear, has been for too long.

Many people predicted, discussed, and described exactly what's happening today. Spoken, written, blogged, recorded on audio and video devices. Intuitive channels warned of this day. The ancients told us. How did they know? They didn't even have phones, let alone the Internet. Weird!

Planning vs Preparing

Why didn't we listen? Why didn't we understand what to do, before the tsunami hit? Most if not all of the humans I know seem to have had no idea what to do to plan for this highly anticipated and predicted System Fail.

Me, too. Oddly, I felt something like this heading towards us, as recently as three years ago. I was quite the Nervous Nelly, but had no evidence what would happen. Although I've always had a (very small scale) gift of foresight and prediction, I just couldn't envision what, how, or when.

The tsunami warning bell going off, incessantly, drove me a little crazy, but no wave big enough to reach ME (privileged and protected) hit the shore, until now.

I could not figure out what to do because I wasn't receiving sufficient information about why, when, where, or how it would unfold. I did ASK. Truly. I prayed. I listened within, and I searched the vast Interwebs regularly for hints, clues, signs, guidance. It's kind of my job to stay current. But, nope. Nuthin. Thanks for that, Universe. Not helpful!

Well, It's Here. Now.

I didn't prepare for a prolonged economic collapse as much I would have liked. I lost a lot of sleep and my faith in my purpose was badly shaken. I felt as if the light bulb that had been me, brightly shining in dimly lit rooms since I was quite young, was reaching the end of its lifespan. Soon I might blink out. Unfinished. Unfulfilled. Derailed. So damn ANGRY, too.

In the last two years, I've experienced more health crises (my own & my husband's) than at any time in the last decade. Adding to that challenge, I felt deeply betrayed by the resurfacing conversation around a culture that ignores, dismisses, and devalues the voices of women, of children, of elders, of survivors of rampant abuse. Me, too. Me, too. (That is a tale for another day; I refuse to keep it buried any more. Our stories help us live.)

I won't list everything that's happened to my husband and me, but it was rough, and I got SERIOUSLY scared. I am a Wellness Adventure Tour Guide. I teach this stuff. But nothing I knew helped, and I was forced to return to the medical infrastructure for both me and my husband. It was not nice.

For whatever reason, I was tossed back into the quicksand of pain, despair, immobility, and terror, not to mention serious cognitive deterioration, AGAIN.

I couldn't do much to fix it except sleep. 15-18 hours a day. I felt ashamed, but I couldn't do anything else.

Not healthy. Not helpful. Not hopeful.

Not at all like the 'new' me of the past eight or nine years. Since I figured out at least SOME of the reasons why I'd been so ill most of my life, I'd been living my life like every day is my last. I figured stuff out, got better, and started making up for lost decades bedridden, babying my body, in excruciating pain, for too damn long. (See my chapter in Heal V1 for a brief rundown on that. Good times, yeah.)

Immense waves of grief surfaced. Many layers. I could not avoid or escape the memories. They came at me 24/7, and I just laid there, sick, raging, HORRIFIED at my own behavior, and that of so many in my life who purported to love me. I was up to my ass in memory alligators swimming in stinky pond water. I called myself a Swamp Creature. The shame almost took me out. My whole life was a lie.

Even with all I'd learned about getting better and stronger, about restoring my physical, emotional, and spiritual function after a ridiculously long list of health challenges (that typically scare people when I list the experiences, let alone actually talk about them), I felt marooned, feeling confused, and helpless, wondering why this was happening...

I reluctantly honored the apparent court-ordered lockdown of the past few years because... I don't think I had a choice. No more avoiding the past. I think I had to drop the old, ancestral drama to get to the next stage of the Game.

This experience, now that I know what was about to happen, profoundly served, helping me release the vestiges of that which was keeping me stuck. It felt like it would never end. I kept praying. A lot. People showed up. The angels whispered. I started feeling a little bit better, even though things remain shaky and confusing to this day.

It underscores my suspicion that most of us (yes, me, too), don't know how to cope with changes we can't see or understand. The invisible influences and the tiny little virus buggers get in and we just don't even know what to do.

We can prep, and I did, a little, but long-term planning even for everyday occurrences, seems like the purview only of the MOST organized folks, of whom I am not one. I can say why, but I would bore you. So I will give the headlines:

- Health crises.
- Auto collisions.
- Sudden illness.
- Job loss.
- Obvious symptoms of undiagnosed conditions unaddressed.

So much has happened, my whole life; sometimes several somethings at once. I thought I'd gotten myself better. But no. This ridiculous rollercoaster ride continued.

It amped up the last three years. And consequently, despite my vows and promises to myself and others that I would start doing what needs doing (wills, DNRs, legal stuff most people don't have in place), I am no more ready to weather this long-anticipated global shock wave than I was 20 years ago, when I couldn't get out of bed for two years.

I know lots of people in my situation, who prep as best they may, but... they too are sick, underfunded, and ill. With very little social support, in financial trouble. It's been a challenge trying to help others when I can't even help myself.

Snapping Into Focus

It is amazing to me how the clarity has jumped into hyperdrive, now that people are dying suddenly, weirdly, and painfully, getting really really sick from an invisible viral invasion. It's not like we have no experience with this. Far worse plagues have darkened many a door.

But the economic situation: rickety and underfunded social support, dilapidated, inefficient, cruelty-based 'health care' systems, along with the unprecedented age wave of older and sicker people, far more than ever in history, has doomed most of us with inadequate infrastructure in place to provide decent care, housing, or even a minimal quality of life. For most vulnerable populations in so-called normal times, we are now threatened by yet another bug that might collapse the entire structure, like that hospital in China that fell down just last week.

The entire world has been changed, in just a few months. I won't offer any theories about how, why, or when this situation unfolded. That story will be told one day by smarter people than me. Probably 20 years from now, like always.

The facts are obvious. But the agenda still needs a bit of a polish, so we can figure out what we must do. Folks have been trying to demand accountability, but apparently that, as well as planning, is not really the priority. For me, when the news began to surface about that tiny little bug ravaging parts of China, I felt this WHOMP of understanding, recognition, and concern.

Hoo boy. It's here. It's happening.

After three years of feeling bewildered, cut off, and truly lost, I got the picture. To my chagrin, I wasn't on top of it much in advance, but I knew it was going to be major a few weeks before the world started seeing what I was worrying about.

I did what I could to 'prepare.' However, I don't have storage and my physical challenges preclude my capacity to live very long anyway without the wonderful conveniences of the overly luxurious first world life. That's just my take. I could surprise myself, as I have any number of times in the past 30 or 40 years, but this part of the adventure, I am not so certain how I will navigate. If I am meant to figure it out, I will.

I am sanguine. I have made my peace with living peacefully and unafraid of every possible outcome. Living life as a sensitive Empath can be distressing, and I have had my share of fearful, anxiety ridden nights. And days. I teach people how to deal. I deal.

But I have something to say, and there are others saying this in different ways, and the book I hope you're reading right now is a very good place to say it in my own words. So I will say it in the light of the clarity I have sought for so long.

Human Beings are Resilient

Almost to the point of being TOO successful at surviving major conflict, war, famine, and environmental destruction of one sort or another.

All the wars. All the despots. All the insanity of controlling politicians and greedy oligarchs.

Back a bit further.

Extinction events. Meteor strikes. Ice ages. Possibly, previous civilizations imploding due to technological overreach. I've heard rumors, anyway.

All of this cataclysm has happened for millenia. To humans. Much of it in the past 200 years, we have done to ourselves. The suffering is incomprehensible, unfathomable. But we have survived as a species, and our numbers have exploded.

Together

Humanity has expanded its reach (and its grasp) to the point where we are now hosting a very big party with something like 7.7 billion human bodies inhabiting this tiny, sparkling jewel of life-giving beauty. The predictions model up to 9 billion soon. There is still plenty of room, if we share smartly. Very doable, just not how we've BEEN doing it all.

Not only are we as a species still here, we have each other now, in a way that would boggle the minds of people just 50 years ago. Heck, it boggles MY mind, and I've only recently achieved elderhood.

Until the internet either fails or is shut off, we have each other. And then we will still have each other because we are a lot.

Why not a good future?

I am inviting you, if you wish, to engage deeply, daringly, and determinedly, to say what you see, to begin envisioning your future the way YOU DESIRE IT, because so much has been knee-capped from our access.

If the structure is going down, we might as well start building systems that serve us best. It's not a good time to give up.

We were MEANT for this. We were BORN for this. We have gathered information and remembered that we are so, so powerful WITHIN.

And we are incrediby resilient; maybe almost TOO resilient. I believe *resilience is our superpower* because we still have things to learn.

- To relate to each other as if we even exist.
- To truly, humbly listen to, and respond to each others' needs.
- To fill in each others' empty kettles: food and shelter and our inner and outer need for healing.

We are amazing, wondrous beings of light.

So I have been told. So I see. Despite the crazy behavior, we as a species are incredibly complex and fascinating. Survival is another superpower I think we can depend upon.

Did you know that?

I've known it. For most of my life. But we darken our soul expression and we give up a lot, and we find ways to distract ourselves from all the suffering. I do it too.

But now? I don't think there's a way back to 'before,' to living comfortably numb. Ignoring people lying in the streets, hungry and ill. We are in an irreversible crisis situation, where the weakness of what we have paid so dearly for is obvious to almost everyone.

The only way through this crisis is to rely on our undeniable resilience and our trusty companion superpowers: Compassion, Creativity, and Connectedness.

TOGETHER, we can make a choice. And a radical change.

It IS up to us.

Now that I know what was about to wash over us, I have thoughts. I am not saying anything you haven't already heard on Facebook. I will just underline a few things I am led to say, today, in this moment of clarity.

> **T**ruth.
> **R**espect.
> **U**nderstanding.
> **S**upport.
> **T**ransparency.

- Life is SHORT. Play NICE. This is not just a bromide. It's important.
- Savor every moment and hold the light within you aloft for all to see.
- You are the one we have been waiting for.
- You are the superhero of this virtual reality video game.
- You were born, you are here for this! And you are not alone.

You are as ready as you will ever be, like all the humans of the recent millennia who maybe didn't expect they had it in them to survive the many incursions on their peaceful, gentle lives. Your ancestors did that. You can too.

I invite you to *remember* where you came from, and what you learned despite the steep price, but also, to make peace with your past, and to embrace the unknowable, ineffable, imaginary future. The one you are writing today.

I will remember with you that *Resilience is Our Superpower.*

We got this.

I offer, also, a gift for you. It was given to me, and I am guided to pass it along.

A still small voice whispered this to me a few decades ago. It helps me remember to cherish every moment.

So simple. So sweet. So SUPERHERO:

Love *TODAY*.

You are in charge now. And your inherent resilience will save us all. I appreciate that in you. I appreciate that in you. I honor the Joyous Journey we share, as we figure this part out. TOGETHER. TODAY.

THANK YOU.

A natural-born intuitive, empath, telepath, clairvoyant, and sound healer, Ashara delivers enlightening angel card readings, awakening abundance activations, and a myriad of healing modalities to those who seek Visionary Insight and Sound Guidance.

Areas of Service:

Wellness Adventure Tour Guide: Sensible, cost-effective, non-invasive, integrative wellness strategies and referral resources for chronic illness and pain survivors.

Emerging Empath Entrepreneur Empowerment: Creative strategies, divinely guided connections, and inventive solutions for sensitive business owners.

Literary Doula & Word Weaver: Enthusiastic cheerleading, gentle developmental editing, and confidence building, fostering an encouraging container for aspiring writers.

UPspiralling *You* from Status Quo to Status GLOW.

Ashara Love | Phone: 206-905-1055 | Skype: CreatrixConnexion
Email: info@creatrixconnexion.com | creatrixconnexion.com

A Momentous Metamorphosis

By Audrey Lingg-Bertoni

My wish for you is to take the time to just 'be.'

Invest the time to 'be' in nature, 'be' with family, 'be' doing what you love to do! If I had it to 'do' over again, I wouldn't wait until my body, mind, and soul enforced what I needed and wouldn't 'do' for myself, which was to just 'be.'

Ever start a year and say "What the f**k is happening here? Am I the only one to ever experience this...?"

By the end of 2018 my body was broken, my mind splintered. I was financially ruined, spiritually shattered, and I had left a trail of broken relationships in my wake. Taking all of this into the following year, I was not in great shape. I must confess 2019 was a hell of a year!

The year started off with downsizing to one quarter of the possessions I owned, abandoning my house for minimal financial gain, selling or giving away most everything I owned, and storing the rest in my son's garage.

The Higher Powers were taking care of me, helping me get rid of responsibilities that my subconscious instinctively knew I wouldn't be able to handle during that year of crazy. That was the only way I knew how to acknowledge I was physically exhausted: my body ached all the time. I had pain where I shouldn't because I wasn't doing anything difficult, nothing close to the hard physical work I was used to.

I didn't feel like doing anything – just felt like sitting and not thinking. I didn't have the physical energy to even get out of bed, but I made myself get up. Eating was an effort, but I made myself food and ate it. The exhaustion was even in my eyes, which I can only describe as a 'tired' ache. I just wanted to close my eyes and rest forever.

I knew that this was not normal! Have you ever felt in your gut that there is something seriously wrong, but didn't know what it was? I made myself search for answers, but in my confused mental state, the decision-maker part of me couldn't make sense of even the simplest of decisions. I felt disoriented, like I'd been suddenly tossed into water and I didn't know which direction was up...

What was familiar to me – over-caring and over-helping in any relationship I was in – became impossible to do anymore... I thought I had been keeping my life together, I thought... lots of things like that, until that time... but then, the next level of transition started to take shape.

I was done with looking after anybody but me. Still, it took time for that realization to surface into clarity, to become fully visible into my conscious awareness. After all, "…isn't it selfish to just look after myself?" But I'd had it; everything felt like it was coming at me all at once, and I couldn't handle anything anymore. Lashing out emotionally… in anger, crying in despair, or sometimes collapsing, slumping down in defeat. I was not able to stop myself from feeling and expressing and revealing all these emotions. Gone were the days when I could hold them all in, like 'normal.' Even though on the outside it seemed I had it all together, I was broken inside.

It took a long time to move the 'Emotional Titanic,' but the iceberg was lurking… I never saw it coming.

These long-simmering mental and emotional hurts actually began before I was even born… Shortly after my mother's dad passed away, she was raped, and that's how I came to be. Born to a 14-year-old single mom, growing up in a very small town, living with my favourite uncle and my grandmother, I was allowed to let my strong personality shine through.

When I reached the age of seven, my mother got married. I was so excited to have a whole family experience and to even have a 'dad.' But my mother's new husband had demons of his own and I was soon experiencing sexual abuse at the hands of the man I thought would protect and love me. The sexual abuse lasted well into my teen years, leaving wounds and hurts that would affect my whole family for many years to come, and still do, even to this day.

My outspokenness that used to make the older men of the town laugh soon disappeared. A shadow was cast over my light, and I withdrew from being the bright and exuberant child I had been. I often found myself running down to the creek behind the church, to hide, to escape. It became my safe place, where no one could find me. I'd be calmed by the trickling water. When I'd finally go back home, I would help my mother. Take over household chores and care for my siblings – whatever kept me too busy to feel…

These things, buried deep in my past, were often at the surface of my present, scratching at my mind, wanting to be let out.

The yearning to escape from these hurts was embedded in my soul, and my urge to run, to hide, and escape became progressively worse. But, that's not where this story is going to go. That whole situation is a story for another time.

This particular story is a tale of what happens when those mental and emotional hurts go unresolved for far too long. This is where my body, mind, and spirit took over, their infinite wisdom taking me into the deepest darkest night of my soul…

Summer 2019, I ended up in Kelowna, living in my car with my only companion and confidante, my cat. Stinky was my soul companion. During times when I was really low, Stinky would stay close, watching over me; she was my guardian angel, and her presence kept me going. From everyone else, I was hiding out emotionally and physically.

My greatest times in Kelowna were when I'd locate a spot along the Okanagan Lake, put my feet in the water, and just 'sit' there. I'd relax, listen to the waves, feel the water on my skin, and meditate to the pulsing of nature. As night approached, I'd stare into the flames of my campfire – and just 'be.' Then I would sleep, deeply and comfortably, until dawn.

Tuesday nights, there was salsa dancing; I could just 'be' there. Dancing takes me out of my mind. It's easy, it just flows. It's my kind of exercise. My physical body gets what it needs, and I am in a space of just 'being.'

That was a summer of finding that thing that could take me away from my mind, to just 'be' in the individual moment. I realize now that I was very distanced from myself and everybody else. Even dancing, I would just be with me. I didn't have to talk, think, or be in the group, without any obligation to have conversations, for which I am so grateful. It was my summer of monkhood.

Two months into living in my car in Kelowna, night after night I found myself 'running from the law,' as there are rules about where you can park your car and sleep. After finishing work at the fruit stand, I'd head out in my car, full of all my belongings, wanting to find a place to sleep for the night, just to rest. I would drive around, looking for a place where no one would report me to the cops, who would kick me out. By this point, I was beyond exhausted.

I knew I was in a really bad place with my mind, with my body, with my spirit, with my soul. I felt out of control, I felt lost, I felt broken. I was in so much pain. I shoved all of that under the rug, just as my mother used to say when she talked about what had happened to her. It seems I'd forgotten how my response was always to point out that the rug was not big enough to cover all the things spilling out from underneath.

I was asking myself questions: "Is this PTSD or depression or anxiety? Or is it some other mental illness label, or what...?" All I knew was, it was really confusing and definitely not fun. I just knew I was not being myself.

Then my soul companion, Stinky, left me, jumping out of the car when I was not there, never to be seen again. The next day, I found a roof, a door and a BED!

Did Stinky's leaving have anything to do with my finding an affordable place to live? Did the cat-size hole in my heart leave just enough room for me to finally let myself find a safe place? I don't know if Stinky had anything to do with any of that, but it seemed that way. To me, anyway... I miss you, Stinky. Thanks Stinky, for being my driving companion.

Throughout this whole year I had been returning to Edmonton, on and off to see my doctor. I wanted to know what was going on with me. My eyes were still hurting and TIRED. He did a whole bunch of tests, from osteoporosis to arthritis, bone density to iron deficiency. Nothing was coming up. I still felt crappy! My body was still aching and my back was still hurting.

The doctor said, "I can do more tests, but it's just your age. You're in menopause." His words and tone felt dismissive. I was frustrated with his inability to hear what I was saying, and I was taken aback by his lack of acknowledgment that I know my body and what resonates with what I think and feel. I may not have known what was making me feel so bad, but my whole being was telling me what it wasn't – and it wasn't menopause. I was not feeling heard.

I knew he had the results of a urine test and I said, "I wanna know the results. Can I just see the results?" He dismissed me, saying, "They are fine..." I persisted in asking for the results. When he finally opened the report he said, "Oh wow... your white blood count is PLUS 500. IT'S SUPPOSED TO BE 20." Finally a breakthrough; by this point it was January 2020, my pain level was at a twelve out of ten, and my patience was at zero.

What he didn't tell me was that this infection was in my brain already. I learned that from my friend who is a nurse; she told me the toxins were affecting my thinking, reasoning, decision making. How did he miss it? I'd been so tired for months...

My doctor prescribed ten days of penicillin, yet after I finished the full prescription, I still wasn't feeling very well. I was still really confused and slow; and that was when I had a light-bulb moment.

I thought 'Hey, guess what? I'm an aromatherapist. Maybe I should use my own remedies!" I quickly proceeded to put together a capsule combining different Essential Oils containing high antibacterial, antiviral, and anti-inflammatory properties like Oregano, Melaleuca ™, Frankincense, Helichrysum, Copaiba, and On Guard, all of which also boosted my immune system. I took the capsules for three days and, WOW, it was like daylight dawning. My brain was clear and my back stopped hurting. Oh my god, you have no idea how that felt. Before, it was like I was looking at the world through sheer white curtains, and after, it was like the curtains were opened and I could see through the window clearly.

Even though I am still a bit foggy here and there, I am able to have great conversations, I make clearer decisions, and I am feeling more like my original, feisty self.

I don't believe that I was just experiencing a physical infection, although that is how it would be perceived by many. I know my life too well for that. I believe I had to learn how to just 'be.' Before, I had been a 'human doing', doing more than I could handle – for others, without having the energy to do what I needed for myself. It came to a point where the Higher Powers had to shut down both my mental and physical, to force me to just 'be' and in that just 'being,' I found 'me.'

I've learned so much in the last year about myself. For one thing, I was a workaholic; it was always the physical work that I'd escape to, to stay out of my feelings. I have now allowed myself to go into my consciousness to dig deeper for answers. Before I got it handled, I was so confused by the infection in my head/brain/mind that I couldn't go into any of my feelings properly, which made me incoherent and easily agitated.

I'd never felt that way before. I had been a clear-thinking person, spontaneous, able to make a decision on a dime. I could look ten steps ahead of any situation and figure out those steps. I knew I was capable of recovering from the fog and I began to take the steps in healing for my mental wellbeing, one step at a time.

I now have more energy. I know what fuels me, what I need to do to give myself the care I desperately needed. Now I am more aware of who I am, and 'being' more conscious of living my life to the fullest.

The journey doesn't end here... I am constantly learning lessons... but now, I give my body, mind, and spirit the time they need, as I rest and take care of myself.

I am learning new ways to 'be present' in the world; I know I will never end up in such a dark place again. I am becoming a human 'being,' never again to be merely a human 'doing.' That is the ultimate goal of my life right now... Living life to the fullest, in every moment, and being mindful of what makes my body, mind, and soul soar to new joy.

My wish is that you can 'be present' and just 'be' as well.

Audrey Lingg-Bertoni's career – farm hand, construction worker, lifeguard, personal development, aromatherapy, business owner – is multifaceted and fierce, like her. Peeling away the rough layers from her childhood, compounded by the delusion she could handle it all herself, her journey to authenticity demonstrates the power of inner trust, filtered through truthful, raw vulnerability.

Moments in and out of reality transformed her life, shifting her path in momentous ways. Now fearlessly engineering her own destiny, she welcomes FUN, ease, and free-flowing abundance into her life. She'll happily teach you how you can too.

Audrey Lingg-Bertoni
Phone: 780-298-3542 | Email: empoweredlivingacademy@gmail.com

Reset

By Christine Monaghan

RESET practices transform life areas to
Stress is Optional from *Stress is Normal.*

Allowing yourself to ASK, believe, allow, and receive your
truest desires in the highest good of all is your birthright.
RESET commitments, conversations, and choices influence the discovery of your sacred self. Evolving into your
next best version is a gift that allows you to heal and to
contribute to our collective potential.

~ Christine Monaghan, RESET Coach and Consultant

Why RESET?

Oxford Dictionary – *reset something, to place something in correct position again*

RESET is your choice to set again, anew in any moment, hour, day, week, month. How wonderfully liberating and empowering to live each day *knowing* you can RESET in each conversation, commitment, or choice to grow into the next best version of you!

Internal and external RESET practices cultivate well-being in reality, while welcoming potential.

In the moment of awareness of feeling less than positive, re-program your ingrained cellular reactions with RESET practice(s) toward what you do want.

My RESET

In 2004, I owned a national personal development seminar series, with 300+ national and international speakers, taking place in bookstores across Canada. Notable sponsors included: Discovery Health Channel; Chatelaine Magazine; CruiseShip Centers; Miraval Resort, etc. In the expansion phase, I was working with a new business partner, scheduling a tentative Deepak Chopra headline date, and planning a U.S. national magazine collaboration.

Expanding the business included concept development, sponsorship, logistics, and marketing, plus connecting with consultants to support our growth. At this point in my career, I'd raised millions in sponsorship and sales, and co-produced 80k+ attendee world-class sporting and cultural events.

A romance had recently ended, so I decided to heal by training for a half-marathon. Athletic strength and healthy lifestyle were second nature for me since childhood, a daily energizer, and reliable stress release go-to. My only vices were vino and lemon tart treats! But I still didn't feel quite right.

My doctor reassured me that my feeling so off was simply stress – I obviously had a lot on my plate. I'd fought with underlying anxiety, invisible to others, and I treated it with plenty of sleep, exercise, healthy food, and yoga.

On the last day of September, 2004, I ventured off to my biggest career meeting to confirm a million-dollar business investor.

I did it!

Arriving home victorious, I felt bone tired (had for weeks). I shrugged off feeling odd to enjoy sushi and a craft beer. The next 24 hours involved passing out, becoming violently ill, and landing at ER October 1, a gorgeous fall day, thinking, "a perfect Seawall run day!" In hindsight, my roommates' insistence to call 911 was a life-saver.

Post-surgery, I faced a new future. My super healthy, athletic body now sported a pacemaker and a scar. My heart had stopped, and I'd had several out of body experiences. What the eff happened?

I returned home October 2, assured that my heart was still healthy despite a misfiring electrical system compounded by low blood pressure (part genetic, part athletic). This was deemed idiopathic, meaning no known reason. No medication needed, and I was free to sign up for a half marathon, or anything I wanted to continue being a dedicated athlete.

Internal psychological terror and stress warfare surged through me.

I knew I had to address this fear directly. To relearn to trust in my remarkable bio-machine, which had always served me well. But how?

Although my RESET began October 1, 2004, I couldn't articulate it as such just then. Following my near-death experience, I published, *HeartBroke, an Entrepreneur's Journey from Uncertainty to Possibilities*. I originally referred to the shift as 'the Crumble.' Fifteen years forward, I refer to it as my RESET, and feel deeply privileged to introduce my clients to the amazing benefits of implementing its healing power, presence, and potential.

These days, when I share my expertise in RESET coaching and consulting, I'm speaking from having done so for myself. I'd learned that a RESET approach to life is a necessity. I emphasize that when (not if) a life challenge presents itself, the ability to access proven practices will help you confidently navigate through choppy waters with trusted solutions – cultivated with internal source energy.

A clean life canvas can be daunting, but this shock to my system provoked me to grow into the next best version of me. Post October, innate intuition led me to institute habitual moments of RESET: hourly, daily, monthly. I did this in particular to tame my internal *what if* worry associated with my near-death experience. This worry was running the show, exhausting me emotionally, and certainly messing with me psychologically.

I recognized that I had a choice to make. Either learn to accept what took place and utilize it in a positive manner, or slide into a life of containment on all levels. I hadn't achieved and strived to this point to curl up into a ball and cringe. Containment and mediocrity felt like death, so I made the commitment to, once and for all, learn to let go of *what if* worry and use my go-for-it personality to pull forward the best of what I was good at and loved to do – inspiring people to tap into their inherent potential.

I didn't yet fully comprehend my innate capacity to tame *what if* worry and troublesome thoughts, but I started by finding my way to a new level of clarity. I began reviewing every commitment, conversation, and choice, deciding whether to hold onto, expand, or release.

Within weeks of the unscheduled surgery, I realized my best choice was to listen to the loud and clear message. I closed my business, and walked away from my investor plus business partner, to center my focus on RESET.

My RESET commitment? Hourly, daily RESET practices intended to shift perceived and real challenges into fresh opportunities to create! CHOOSING *stress is optional.* There were plenty of tears and moments of fear, but I was resolute that I could be intentional. I held the intention of: The best is yet to come.

I incorporated a number of valuable RESET resources into my new life:

- **Psychological counseling.** This included addressing resurfacing, older trauma. Adding in tapping (Emotional Freedom Technique) exercises was helpful. I didn't believe in tapping until I did it!
- **Daily meditation.** I resisted doing this regularly, but grew to love it.
- **Hired a trainer.** To regain my trust and confidence athletically, I worked with a retired pro-football player personal trainer.
- **Returned to running.** I went to a local park with my chocolate lab to restore my joy.
- **Worked with a life coach.** His humor lifted my spirits and he influenced the professional services I offer today.
- **Got support.** My close circle of pals nudged me back into socializing. So much love!

My conviction? Befriend uncertainty for fresh possibilities.

I navigated physical and psychological fear and loss. Such a huge change to my professional identity. My (perceived) lack of womanly appeal – having a scar from a pacemaker, at age 42, was also destabilizing.

Confronted with a major challenge – having zero interest in business, yet needing revenue – I committed to a paper route, of all things. I walked the route with my dad, a retired judge. This choice was a baby step into my new life, and the time with my dad was a wonderful, reassuring balm.

How these unusual choices helped me RESET:

- Instilled responsibility and routine, quieting anxiety.
- Supplied money to pay those helping me heal forward.
- Rebuilt my upper body strength from the cut chest muscle.

Many of the RESET practices I turned to while recovering from surgery now influence others in the midst of choice and change. Who knew? I was becoming a RESET Coach and Consultant!

RESET practices source innate intelligence to influence yourself and others going forward. Feeling connected and alive provides profound access to healing states.

Commitment to RESET practices gives you a choice to HEAL FORWARD in any given moment.

> Do not be dismayed by the brokenness of the world.
> All things break, and all things can be mended.
> Not with time, but with intention. So go. Love.
> Intentionally, extravagantly, unconditionally. The broken
> world waits in darkness for the light that is you.
> ~ L.R. Knost, feminist

By stepping into this newly embraced, innate gift of checking in, connecting, and resetting my perspective, my coaching and consulting vision evolved. I began moving forward to support individuals who desire to move from a *stress is normal* to a *stress is optional* daily life experience.

Stress is optional is a term that provokes you to consider your current mental attitude. Power in choice is a human being's privilege. You can't control what others do or the external situations you may be facing. Mindful choice, combined with RESET practices, creates a powerful container for solutions for all kinds of situations to show up.

Commitment to RESET practices; becoming a Stress is Optional leader.

When we make the commitment to RESET, we're taking the first step to move from a *stress is normal* to *stress is optional* approach to life. I learned, and I began teaching others how to RESET. The inner shift is really powerful once you've incorporated it into your daily life.

My clients have shared their experiences:

Christine is a no nonsense coach who can help you to rise from the ashes. Within minutes, she had me regrouped, refocused, the anxiety had gone away and I had the RESET tools to get the job done. Chris really "shows up" for her clients by getting to the problem and creating immediate solutions. I went to her when I was ready to quit. She pulled me out from the dark hole I was in and got me back on track. Within one month, I had surpassed my financial goals and had a record breaking month after 5 years of being in business! Thank you Chris for being an angel guiding me back to the light!
~ DeeAnne Riendeau, Founder, Your Holistic Earth

I came to know of Christine Monaghan through BC CPHR's professional development opportunities. The session I attended was the The 3C's of Communication; 10 RESET Solutions-Based Tools. I attended this webinar with no expectations, thinking it would be your typical communication workshop. I was really surprised by the content of the material. It was not what I expected.

Christine raises the awareness that how we communicate is how we manage our time, and our stress. In today's world, we think stress is the norm. Christine emphasizes that stress is optional and provides tools on how we communicate and how we commit to our communications.

It was such an invigorating webinar that I introduced Christine to my workplace and she presented two webinars so far. I never thought I would be one to work with an accountability and career coach, but I have now signed up with Christine and am going through a self-discovery process which is both challenging and exciting at the same time. I can't wait to see the end results!

~ Dawn Ng, HR Manager

I worked with Christine to help me get unstuck from a few years of procrastination and uncertainty about where I wanted to live and buy a home. By following Christine's logical RESET steps and tools, it took away overwhelm and within just a few months I was able to finally make the move to a new city where there is a lot more opportunity for me to achieve my life goals.

~Catherine A, Vancouver

Your RESET is TODAY

I have great news! There is no need for you to experience a life-altering situation or challenge to begin cultivating a *stress is optional* RESET approach. Cultivate it NOW, so you will be well equipped when inevitable challenges arise. Internal liberation and freedom is our birthright, accessible when we give ourselves permission to RESET.

Life is way more light-hearted and productive with source energy generating co-creating results that were once masked in resistance and struggle.

When you are ready to experiment with this simple-to-implement process, I've detailed the tools in a series of books:

- *Why RESET?*
- *Slow Down to Move Ahead*
- *Why Can't I Just Focus?*

RESET practices become your *go-to solution* when you reach moments of awareness: of overwhelm, stress, frustration, negative thoughts, sensations.

Start with *slowing down to move ahead*. Slowing down to move ahead goes against the acceptable, conditioned norm. Society is programmed to demand that we speed up, multi-task, get more, be more, scroll more!

Just so you know, you will feel resistance. Go ahead and assume that resistance will surface when beginning this commitment. It's to be expected that worn-out thoughts and beliefs (habits) won't be happy!

Moment to moment awareness is mindfulness, where you begin to make a choice to replace negative internal or external triggers with commitments, conversations, and choices in the highest good for all.

Choosing to pause reminds you of the power you have to support a *stress is optional* stance. The RESET pause allows your nervous system to return to its natural state of ease. Each pause literally re-programs your cellular system. One of many additional benefits is topping up your energy reserve.

As you slow down to move ahead, you free up time, space, and energy to intentionally work ON versus IN your life, creating the next best version of you. De-cluttering your mind, sort of like when you defrag your computer hard drive. My ebook, *Why Can't I Just Focus?* helps you learn how.

Attention is the rarest and purest form of generosity.
~ Simone Weil, philosopher

Since you've read this far, would you like to get started?

RESET Exercise:

Now that I've shared some good reasons why you might wish to experiment with the RESET practices, here is a way to begin co-creating your own *stress is optional* RESET commitment for daily practice:

Ponder those unwelcome, unpleasant moments of stress, overwhelm, underwhelm, boredom (fear), or procrastination.

What distractions or old habits kick in during your day, more often than not?

Now, list the <u>top three distractions</u> that tend to surface in moments of stress or overwhelm, maybe two or more times weekly.

1.

2.

3.

Next, list <u>two feelings</u> these distractions trigger that seem to work against you pursuing your desires.

1.

2.

Terrific!

Now, take a moment or two and IMAGINE you've conquered these three distractions.

Ask yourself this question: What's the #1 success habit responsible for my quantum leap, 12 months from today? (HINT: It's the opposite of the distractions.)

Create a one sentence reminder to represent this #1 success habit, IN THE PRESENT TENSE, as though you've implemented it fully over the past year.

Example: I make commitments I can fulfill with ease to positively influence goal-achieving.

When you ask these kinds of questions, it is ASTONISHING what your mind will tell you. Did you get something?

Your # 1 Success Habit:

_____

Amazing! You've just created your first RESET commitment!

More RESET Solutions

Implement your customized RESET practice with simple, proven principles, tips, tools, and exercises that provide powerful solutions for lasting results!

RESET ebooks. These easy-access books offer a terrific reference for leaders to incorporate in their own life and to powerfully influence successful team growth and mental well-being.

- *Why RESET?*
- *Slow Down to Move Ahead*
- *Why Can't I Just Focus?*

Reset2020now.com

RESET NOW. Quick Start Gifts for you.

Gift #1

7-Day RESET Planner. stressisoptional.thinkific.com/courses/free-7-day-reset-planner

Gift #2

Experience your transformative introductory RESET 45-minute 1:1 coaching call. ChristineMonaghan.com/free-2

Choices with Christine

Consider working with me one-on-one, or for team building and empowerment.

About Christine Monaghan: Reset2020now.com | christinemonaghan.com

Christine is your human-potential champion! When you understand the power and simplicity of the RESET approach, you can ramp up to source your next level of potential in all areas of your life.

Christine's work with individuals and organizations is solution-based with a 100% focus on establishing and achieving foundational goals. Clients experience a complete RESET: clarity in what they really, really want; focused productivity for profit; consistent goal-achieving; a *stress is optional* daily experience.

She shares her eclectic business and life acumen; skilled implementation of powerful methodical systems; and the life-altering practice of focusing on the 3C's – commitments, conversations, and choices – to easily access the results you desire.

Christine's RESET vision for you:

Fresh vibrancy, opportunities, and results, as she gently guides you through resistance, fear, and old habits to deliver you smoothly from where you are today to where you crave to be.

Christine's pre-RESET background: producing 80K attendee, world-class events; raising millions of dollars in sponsorship/sales; coordinating national corporate launch promotions; and building a 4-city personal development series in collaboration with Discovery Health Channel and Chatelaine magazine. After her near-death experience, she left her business, wrote a book, and developed tools for her own RESET.

With 15+ years experience as a RESET Coach and Consultant, Christine is your GO-TO RESET COACH, nudging you through resistance, fear, and old habits to adopt a RESET life of fresh vibrancy, opportunities, and results. A master motivator, Christine influences the next best version of you.

Christine Monaghan | Email: choiceswithchris@gmail.com
Reset2020now.com | ChristineMonaghan.com

A Path to Meaning

By Dave Sinclair

In 2012, I found myself waking up in a cold, dark, windowless detention cell. I was alone, with a pounding headache, at 41 years old.

What the hell was going on? Why was I here? Then the pieces of the previous night came back, slowly and painfully.

The party. Getting blackout drunk. The cops showing up.

My family and I were out of town with my son's hockey team for a tournament. It was supposed to be a great family time. But instead, I had tried, yet again, to escape stress by drinking, and I got out of control.

Waking up, locked in that cell, helped me face the truth: something was seriously wrong.

How did I go from business success to a drunk in a cell? Why was I turning family trips into hardcore drunken party nights? Was it the stress? Or was it something more?

Sitting in my cell, I began to grasp that it was more than stress. I had numbed myself to the fact that I'd lost touch with my values. I was unsure who I really was anymore.

I didn't like that feeling. I wanted to change.

Nothing like a drunk tank cell to help me viscerally feel what I had been trying so hard to avoid: my loss of connection, identity, and values.

There had to be more to life than this. I couldn't keep sleepwalking through life, but I didn't know what the 'more' meant, nor did I have any idea how to connect with what was important to me: my values and identity.

One thing I was pretty sure of, as I faced the wreckage caused by my recent life choices, was that this was not going to be an easy, quick fix to changing my life. It was going to take a lot of work.

Change Takes Work

No one goes from living a perfect, stress-free life to ending up in a drunk tank overnight. The muck builds up over time. The same principle applies the opposite way: no one goes from living a stress-filled life to an entirely happy one overnight.

Real Change Takes Real Work

For example, entrepreneurs always look to take their business to the next level or to turn their business around so they can have more time. However, if they aren't clear on the vision and values they want for their business and life, they often spin their wheels.

It is fine to want to earn money, but in this transformational business atmosphere, it's essential to know what matters to you, and why.

I have seen too many entrepreneurs look for quick fixes that will help their company transform. They spend thousands on books, seminars, and conferences, but often obtain limited results. They momentarily feel inspired and take a couple of small steps forward, but when the next emergency comes up (there are ALWAYS emergencies in business), the focus is dropped.

Developing Solid, Supportive Habits for Real Success

If struggling entrepreneurs don't change their habits for the long run, their situation just resets to what it was before. Entrepreneurs looking for a magic formula or plan to turn their business into a success overnight will consistently experience a sense of hopelessness.

Chasing money for money's sake never brings happiness

Change, no matter its form, takes work, and it's a process. There is no instant magic formula that works. None of us live in a Hollywood movie.

Instant success is as likely as winning the lottery. Real success for an entrepreneur's business starts when they get clear on what they actually want the money, growth, happiness, and prosperity for.

Changing habits and creating growth starts by taking a step back and deciding what is important to you and what you value inside and outside of your business.

Spending More Won't Make You Happy

Looking back on my life, I fell into a great job. I rose from apprentice to manager to part-owner at a multinational company. From the outside, I was successful. A big house, fancy cars, and expensive vacations. I had all the materialistic items that I thought should make someone like me happy. But I wasn't. It was all superficial.

I learned this the hard way: The pursuit of physical items never fully satisfies our desire for happiness. It results in temporary joy, but that happiness rarely lasts longer than a few days.

The materialistic items I had accumulated are not bad things, but they can cause problems if used to define success, which is exactly what I did.

All I made time for outside of work was escaping, by buying things and looking for the next party. I thought being in the office for 80+ hours a week and making more money would lead to success in life. I want you to know, I tried the escape hatch, better toy, and bigger drink route.

I was 70lbs overweight, my relationship with my family was rocky, my blood pressure was sky high, and I drank too much. I was not healthy, mentally, or physically. Work had consumed my life. I judged myself harshly about who I WASN'T, instead of stepping into who I was and wanted to be.

I had no idea there was a better life to live. I was mentally blind, and had no idea how having, defining, or embracing values that mattered to me could change my experience in my workplace, let alone my life.

I had to learn that happiness is not defined by what we own, or what we imbibe, but what we value. In that cell, I at least recognized I needed to do something different.

Quitting Didn't Solve My Problems

Initially, I blamed all my problems on work. So in 2011, I quit. I got bought out and left behind my uncomfortable life as a partner in a multinational company. I was out of the business that I thought was the main root of all my problems. Surprising to me, the stress, unhappiness, and drinking continued.

Why? Because work had become my identity. I didn't know who I was outside work. Once I gave up what I thought was the root cause of my unhappiness, I discovered that I was now even more lost than before.

If business/work was NOT where my stress really came from, what was I supposed to do? I had no emails to answer, no team, no schedule. I began to face the big questions. Starting with: Who am I?

How I Turned My Life Around

"Change doesn't happen overnight. There's no button
that's pushed to magically alter everything.
Change happens little by little. Day by day. Hour by hour."

~ J.M. Darhower

Quitting was not the answer to achieving happiness. Building an identity and discovering my values was required. I didn't yet know how, but I knew I had to learn.

After waking up in a cell, I knew I wanted to change for good. I wanted to feel full, valued, and happy. I thought about what I hadn't yet accomplished. My questions changed from the inside: Where do I go from here? What do I want my final storyline in life to be about?

The guidance started to show up soon after I reached out for help. A key pivot forward happened during my time at a meaning and purpose addictions recovery center, as I read Victor Frankl's book, *'Man's Search for Meaning.'* Frankl's book got me to question my life and kick-started my journey to discover a more meaningful way of living.

Frankl was a survivor of Nazi concentration camps. He went through hell, but his experience helped him see how, as Nietzsche said, "He who has a why to live for can bear with almost any how."

He believed that many people suffered from a lack of meaning, causing them to be unhappy. From his time in the death camps, to developing *logotherapy* and helping countless clients, he found that when people were able to uncover meaning in their lives, they could find happiness and flourish. He observed that meaning and happiness came about as a result of the things we do and the experiences we have.

Frankl explained that meaning comes about in three main ways:

1. We can find meaning in the work we do and the things we accomplish.

2. We can find meaning in experiences such as finding the beauty in nature, appreciating art, loving others, etc.

3. We can find meaning in our suffering, if there is nothing we can do to remove that suffering. If we can remove that which is causing the suffering, do so. If we can't, Frankl suggests we change our minds about how we see it.

Frankl recommended that instead of chasing happiness as a goal in itself, it's essential to connect with what is important to you and then work towards setting goals, doing things, and having experiences that in and of themselves feel important to you. Happiness and a deeper sense of meaning will naturally result as you engage with these goals or activities.

Something More For Me

I instinctively knew there was something more for me in this life. However, I'd never find it if I didn't take the time to step back and answer what it is that I actually want. When I took that much-needed step back, everything started to fall into place.

> I wanted to run marathons, grow a company that didn't consume me, become closer to my family, and have genuine connections with people and my community.

After defining my actual values and identity, my clarity provided a map for my turnaround. I took my MBA, obtained a certification in exit planning, and became certified as a professional coach.

Achieving this success on the inside could never happen overnight. It took a lot of work. But getting through it all and finding my happiness prompted me to start a business to help my clients achieve the same success and satisfaction. I find meaning by inspiring clients to change their lives sustainably and with purpose.

I want to see others achieve the same success I gained after I did the work and found meaningful happiness.

The First Step To Change

Once you sense what you want your life to be like, you can look at where you are right now, and start taking action. Having a vision of your ideal life helps you align your actions and choices.

Taking a step back is the first phase of finding happiness and changing your lifestyle. To help you get started, I've created a 4-stage step back process that can be used for almost any aspect of your life you want to improve or change.

These 4 stages can help you go from, "I don't know what the future holds," to a feeling of, "I know what I want the future to look and feel like, and I have a plan to make this a reality!"

Stage One

Feeling stuck is normal. The first step to getting unstuck is believing you can learn and grow. I sure remember how stuck I felt that morning in the detention cell. Literally and figuratively. I'd never felt so trapped.

What if, instead of sinking into the stuck, you said, "This is where I am, and this is what got me here." What if you went a step further, and said, "With what I've learned so far, and knowing I want change, I know I can learn, I know I can grow, and I know I can move forward."

The critical concept of a growth mindset is what allowed me to start getting unstuck.

> Growth mindset: cultivating the belief
> that you can learn and grow.

You don't have to accept you are stuck where you are. Instead, you can continually break through your self-imposed limitations by being open to new ideas, new habits, new ways of learning, and by putting in the effort to move forward.

Being honest with yourself about where you are and what got you there is half the battle. Committing to the work ahead to make the change is the other half. Once you commit, you're ready to move forward.

Stage Two

You've decided it's time for a change. So what do you want that change to be?

Generating a vision of what you want your future self to be like requires you to focus on tapping into living a life full of meaning and purpose. Create a vision that fills you with HOPE.

Stage Three

So now you know where you are, and you know where you want to go. Great. You're all set, right? Well, you have some idea of the direction, but how about the road map and the fuel to get you there?

Stage Three is where you map out the steps you need to take to get you aimed towards living that ideal life. To help you on your way, you'll need a couple of tools for your rucksack.

Values

Your *Values* allow you to understand how you want to live every day and what is important to you in your core.

Passion

Passion is essentially the gas in your rocket ship. When you choose to live each day more authentically to what you *Value*, a passionate connection to your values will fuel your desire and commitment to do the small things every day that create a better version of yourself as compared to yesterday.

Purpose

As you start uncovering the different aspects of your vision and set objectives for each element that you would like to master, *Purpose* will coalesce into a power center that allows you to tap into your unique constellation of goals.

Plan

Based on the different objectives you've laid out in your vision, the *Plan* helps you tackle larger projects that, when completed, will move you closer to your goals.

Perseverance

Combine your clarity in *Values* with a newfound sense of *Passion* and *Purpose* with the *Plan*, and you find the last key concept from this stage. *Perseverance*. Perseverance is the experience of doing something even though it would be easier not to do it. Perseverance is its own reward. It builds muscle for your journey.

Values, Passion, Purpose, Plan, and Perseverance
all come together to help you push forward!

Stage Four

By Stage Four, you're taking action. Congratulations! It's important to understand that the journey will likely take some time and may not always go smoothly. You will need to keep track, because your journey will inevitably present you with starts and stops, wrong turns, successes and failures.

Below are some qualities and tools to nurture yourself with, so you can enjoy yourself a little more along your path.

Patience is a key quality to develop, so you can maintain your focus as you travel the road to your dream life. Accept that the path is going to be long, and it won't always be clear. Patience allows us to step into the *here and now* more gracefully. It gives us the inner fortitude to be a bit easier on ourselves as we begin to step forward. This is key to the process.

Gratitude allows us to appreciate the work we've done, the things we've learned, and what we already have in front of us.

Write your thoughts. To keep on track and continue following these steps, I recommend keeping a journal. The simple act of writing your thoughts down has wide-ranging benefits: from de-cluttering your mind, to tracking your progress, to encouraging you to set your targets for the day, as you move towards your ideal life.

Happiness is not any one single thing or specific destination. Through my experience, I find happiness to be a verb, as it is something created consciously and continuously in the doing of it. We gain happiness by finding meaning in our actions and experiences as we progress and adjust towards a destination that is aligned to our values in support of our identity.

Happiness is found in living the journey true to yourself.

Finding Your Way

Where am I now? I am happy, healthy, and more fulfilled than ever before. I run marathons, and I'm currently training for an ultra. I love my wife more than ever, and we have a close group of friends with whom to grow inwardly and outwardly.

Traveling for the experience of learning is now a massive part of my life. Most importantly, I have a clear picture of what I want my life to be like. I know what my values are and how to lead with my authentic self. Everything I now do is led with meaning and purpose.

I am proof that there is a better way to live and that you can find happiness. There is a path that can take you from feeling numb to feeling truly present and fully alive. A path to your own unique meaning and purpose.

Are You Next?

I want to make sure you realize something truly important:

> You are not alone. Others feel the same,
> alone and confused about the path forward.

This was a key learning for me. Once I discovered that I was not alone, that help was available, my life started to come back together. You can start your journey anytime; and it doesn't have to start from rock-bottom.

Are you ready to change your life and find happiness? Are you ready to prove the belief that 'success is for those lucky few' is wrong?

Your Pathway to Meaning

Begin by creating your ideal life and business with my Ideal Life Visualization worksheet. This clarifying worksheet is your first step to defining what you want in life – and I mean TRULY want.

Download *The Ideal Life Visualization* worksheet for free today from: davesinclair.ca/ideallife

Dave's mission is to help you stop sleepwalking and start moving towards your ideal state!

Offering a wealth of experience supporting clients in discovering their own pathway to meaning, Dave personally developed the tools he shares to support his business and individual clients in meeting their goals.

Dave holds an MBA. Formerly a partner in a multinational corporation, he is an Exit Planning Professional, a Transition Planning Consultant, a professionally certified coach, and a certified meditation instructor.

Dave coaches:
- People looking for more from life
- Companies looking to improve
- Business owners looking to exit their business

Dave Sinclair | Phone: 780-918-1159
Email: Dave@DaveSinclair.ca | DaveSinclair.ca

What is it Like to Love Yourself?

By Dawn Balash

"Happiness is when what you think, what you say,
and what you do are in harmony."
~ Mahatma Gandhi

For most of my life, I didn't know what self-love was, let alone know that it was possible. Love was always this inaccessible, unachievable state. It was an emotion external to me. Therefore, I kept looking for love in all the wrong places. Every person that I had ever loved rejected me and left me; except of course, my daughter. But that was different; that love was an unconditional love that existed without question. I realized that because I loved my daughter, love was a possibility, a reality, and that I could find love.

About a month before my 38th birthday, unbeknownst to me, reality was sneaking up. I was up-leveling in my coaching business and being "seen" more than I was used to. Add to that, the typical single-parent struggle of time and financial constraints, and the usual work and parental obligations. Ironically, I found myself reverting into hiding from life to avoid the things I just didn't want to deal with. And, with deceptive calmness, I discreetly put my mask on to show the world that all was well on the surface. Just like always.

In the past when I retreated, I was "called out" on my disappearing act; this time was different. Rather than being belittled and emotionally attacked as had happened so many times in my past, this time there was love on the other end. Through that love, I was invited to deal with all of the scary stuff that I had been pushing down. I don't know which was scarier for me: to acknowledge that someone cared enough about me to want to help me deal with my repressed emotions and pain, or dealing with the pain itself! I can say for sure that it was a very fine line.

My initial reaction was to run; run as far as I could away from anybody who cared. It was at this moment that I realized there had been other people who cared about me; who maybe even had loved me. The rush of emotion that flooded out of me came with such force it pushed open a door allowing me the insight that finally, I was ready. For the first time, I felt safe and loved enough that I could, and would, find a way to deal with all of the stuff that was holding me back.

Deal with it? Yes, deal with it. The thing I'd been avoiding, not just at that present moment but all the pain, fears, and guilt that I had been avoiding for the last 37 years. And not just deal with it once and for all, but allow myself to continue to deal with it. Deal. Four simple letters that carry so much weight. Deal. And so much power.

And heal. Dealing with all those repressed emotions, pain, and suffering was actually part of the healing process. Yet, I was in a hurry to get to the healed version of myself. If only I could've skipped over the "dealing with it" phase and move into the healed-and-ready-to-take-on-the-world version of me. I wish I could tell you that it happened overnight; that a fairy flew in and waved her magic wand and I woke up the next morning transformed and healed. That's not how it unfolded at all. I was done living in this fairy tale. I needed to put the fairy tale to rest.

I'd always had this sense of emptiness; not completely full. You know, the glass half-empty, half-full analogy? Well, my internal glass was always half-empty. Always. Since I can ever remember. On the outside, people told me how positive and uplifting I was; how much of a pleasure it was to be around my energy. They commented about how I was so talented and creative in helping so many others who weren't as fortunate as me and how my contagious laughter could change the energy in the room. Half-full. But only on the outside. I wore that mask my whole life. My entire existence was about protecting everything inside me: my internal body, mind, and soul. From what though? What was this mask hiding? I could never quite put my finger on it.

I grew up in a small rural community in northern Alberta, the second oldest in a family of 5, and the only girl. You might think that I had it pretty cushy, with all of that masculine energy around – protecting me, guiding me, modelling for me. It was quite the opposite. My dad was a drinker for as long as I could remember. He worked away from home a lot and when he was physically present, he was never emotionally present.

My mom was a stay-at-home mom who took care of us all as we grew up. She didn't work outside the home and she didn't have, from my perspective as a child, a lot of her own friends. Since my dad was the breadwinner and we didn't have a second vehicle, when he was gone to work, my mom didn't drive. I learned very quickly that women had to rely on men to exist in life: financially, physically, and emotionally. Living in a rural community, I also learned that I should just settle for what I had because the opportunities were very limited. As my brothers got older, my mom began relying on them for various things – more reinforcement for me that women couldn't exist without men taking the reins.

Growing up, our house was a busy place. People coming and going, always a project on the go and every occasion included a few beers. There was a lot of yelling and a lot of unhappiness. Even though I was a smart and very creative kid it seemed I could never be as smart or creative as my brothers – my older brother in particular. I was always following in his footsteps. No matter what I did, it never seemed to be good enough. The one thing I did have going for me however, was my intelligence. I was an honours student, which meant that I could go to university. In fact, I was strongly encouraged to go to university to become a teacher. That's what my dad wanted. However, I wasn't meant to just be a teacher; no, my job was to come home with my degree, marry a farmer and take care of everything in the household. I had no idea that there was another way.

University ended up being a pretty fun time. I found a little tribe that had the same party mindset as me. This was exactly what I was looking for: other people who were also hiding from their past and present realities, using whatever means possible to keep all of their secrets hidden so far down they didn't have to deal with the pain. Oddly enough, I started to live in a world where nobody was good enough for me. No person, no offers of help, no support were good enough. In fact, I refused help when anybody offered it. I started doing everything on my own because since my family's opinion was that I couldn't do anything without a man, I needed to prove to everybody that I could. As usual, I was surrounded by men! Couple that with my parents' fear of me not being taken care of by a man translated into their lack of trust in me. Like my mom who relied on all of the males in our family for most things, I found myself following in her footsteps; both of us kept relying on unreliable men. After so many letdowns and disappointments I truly felt like I had to do everything on my own. I had no choice. In my mind, I knew everything and had to show everybody that I could make it on my own. I was far from perfect but I couldn't let anybody see that.

I truly love taking care of people. I felt called to be responsible to keep others safe from suffering what I went through. Unconsciously, I couldn't help myself, so I made it my life's purpose to take care of others. Instead of following my parents' dream of becoming a teacher, I graduated from university, pregnant, with a BA in psychology. I followed my heart and took care of everyone I could possibly get my hands on: clients within my work, friends, family, strangers, my daughter, as well as in every one of my relationships. Needless to say I didn't become a teacher, nor did I make it back home to marry my farmer.

Despite excelling in high school and then university; working multiple jobs to pay for my education; helping friends and family; in short, putting myself on the line to make others happy, I still didn't feel loved by anyone – not myself, my friends, or my family. And for certain, no man in my life ever made me feel loved. I didn't feel like my parents were ever proud of me. I struggled to fit in even with long-time friends. I couldn't keep a man around long enough to build any kind of connection; the relationships I did build were incredibly unhealthy, emotionally empty, and extremely volatile.

I never felt good enough so I desperately wanted a man. Any man to appreciate me. And to love me. I had all of these gifts. Surely, any man would have done anything to be with a woman like me. I seriously told myself this every day. But why wouldn't they fall in love with me? I couldn't understand any of it. And I just kept looking and seeking and digging myself deeper and deeper into a well of self-pity and victimization. I had no self-worth, no self-confidence, no self-awareness. I was consistently putting myself and my daughter in situations where I thought I was making our lives better; I made more and more futile attempts at finding true love but in the end, I just caused everyone more and more pain.

I was so out of control that the only way I could survive was to be in control of everything. As a result of this need to control things, I suffered from anxiety and panic attacks. However, I was really not in control of anything. I was weighed down by this heavy masculine energy, pushing everyone and everything good in my life away, just so I could keep myself hidden. I really needed to do something different.

Lo and behold, at the age of 34, looking for something more and totally burnt out from being a civil servant, in multiple failed relationships (my longest was 3 years), my many rocky friendships, and uncertainty about the direction of my career, I had done what I always do to cope: I moved – again. Thus began a spiritual journey that created a platform for me to embrace the incredibly painful experience I was to endure over the course of the next 4 years. It was through this journey that I fell in love with myself. Who knew that this was even a thing? What a magnificent, profound experience and knowing for me. It was by loving me that I learned to be a vessel of gratitude and unconditional love.

My life changed so much in those 4 years that I found myself surrounded by true, unconditional love and authentic, warm people who cared so much about me and my emotional and mental wellbeing that I finally felt safe enough to deal with my hurts and pains and underlying self-sabotaging behaviours. One such behaviour that I'd excelled at my whole life was acting as if everything was perfect. I worked really hard to show up that way and was incredibly offended when people would question me and my success. On the outside, no one could see how much pain I was in. No one would ever know how alone I felt despite being surrounded by people... friends, family, coworkers, events, parties, anything I could use to hide behind. I believed that keeping myself busy and being the life of the party was just a tiny defense strategy. Self-protection. No one could hurt me if I kept myself hidden. And I told myself it would only make me stronger. I was so wrong.

When I became pregnant with my daughter it was the most joyous time in my life. She was what I thought I needed to be complete. She came into this world offering me so much and especially, she gave me a way to rebuild my relationship with my family by creating a role where I could feel like I had a purpose. I knew I loved her more than anything I could ever comprehend before she was even more than pea-size big.

I had spent 10 fulfilling years with my daughter; that girl had brought me more excitement, gratitude, love, and joy than I ever thought was possible, and yet I still felt this emptiness inside.

That emptiness came to light on the cusp of my 38th year. After a ton of tears and guilt and judgement and fear, I realized I was tired of hiding and showing up halfway. I was tired of resisting moving forward because someone might actually see me and know me and I wouldn't have to be alone anymore. This may seem like a bunch of disconnected thoughts and feelings that don't even make sense when you say them out loud. But it was loud and clear in my head, and on repeat. Like a broken record. Sound familiar?

The thing is I didn't even know I was ready for this healing. I didn't think it was a problem. It was my excuse for needing alone time. I was emotionally invested in hiding and making excuses. I was an expert at giving distorted, dysfunctional love and expecting something better back – which resonated in the form of validation. As I took the time to feel my fears and blocks and really allowed myself to get through the pain and shadows, I started to see some light. With affirmations all over my house – plastered on my bathroom mirror, phone, calendar, journals, I began to hear a new record to play on repeat.

As I continued building my emotional intelligence and spirituality, I started seeing things in a different perspective. I saw opportunities instead of obstacles. I saw empowerment instead of victimhood. I saw love instead of fear. I started doing things for myself. I started choosing myself first. I started making time for myself. For me. Nobody else. Me. I had no idea how to choose me over anyone else – how selfish would it be to choose me over my daughter, my parents, colleagues, the guy who cut me off in traffic? It was unthinkable to consider that I could choose me over someone else. What I found so liberating was the truth that I was very important in this universe. I was important solely because I was me; not a mom, not a daughter, sister, aunt, friend, professional. Just me. Dawn.

The only way that I could find out how to truly love myself was to love that little girl that was never good enough, that never felt loved, that was forever searching for her happiness. And I did. I let her out to play. I held her. I cuddled her. We laughed together. We played together. I told her how much she was loved and deserved every ounce of being in this magical universe. And she healed. After years and years of loveless loving, she healed. And I healed. I found out what true love was. By loving that little girl inside of me, she was healed. And here's the magical part: in loving that little girl, I learned to love myself in turn. I didn't feel guilty anymore. And I didn't feel lost. I felt whole. That emptiness was gone. I was perfect exactly as I was. As I am. The love that I feel for myself is more heartfelt than I could ever have known or imagined. True self-love.

Loving myself today means that I not only hit the gym, eat consciously, take relaxing lavender baths and stop to smell the roses (of course), but also intentionally take special care of my mind, heart, and soul.

Self-Love. There is no love that could ever replace the love that one has for one's self. Unconditional. Compassionate. Empathetic. And finally I know exactly how it feels.

Dawn Balash is a Self Love, Mindset and Manifestation Coach, speaker and author. She empowers all walks of people to ignite the fire inside by embracing their creativity and boldness through building resiliency and mindset transformation to manifest their epic lives.

Dawn's 18 years experience in human and social services as a Behavioural Specialist and Counsellor has given life to her Coaching today! She is a Certified Life Coach, Neurolinguistic Programming Practitioner (NLP), Certified Ho'oponopono Practitioner, and Access Consciousness Practitioner.

Dawn is mother to an 11-year-old daughter, Lily, and a fur baby, Finnegan, who have been fundamental in her practice as a coach!

You are welcome to the free meditation she shares with her clients that permits access to deeper self love and forgiveness on all levels: www.dawnbalash.com/meditation.

Dawn Balash | Phone: 780-246-0002 | Email: balashdawn@gmail.com

Healing Through Money

How healing your thoughts around money
can change your health and life!

By DeeAnne Riendeau

What does money have to do with your health? A LOT! First, without our health, how can we earn money to have any quality of life? Second, without money, how can we experience a life we want with access to experiences, proper nutrition, and a healthy balance of fun and freedom?

Being sickly was as big a part of my identity as being a middle child. It was always there, always limiting what I could do, limiting the energy I had, visits to the doctor limiting my time, taking medications that limited my freedom, and basically limiting my enjoyment of childhood and my expectations of adulthood. I wanted to be like everyone else – have my shot at being rich and successful. When that came through, it wasn't what I imagined.

I had loving parents, but money seemed to be an issue in our household. We grew up in a small town, on the lower end of middle class, and we never seemed to have extra money for big trips or the nice things we wanted. Dad was very careful with his money, and although we had all we needed, there were things we wanted that we didn't get.

Hearing no a lot, and often feeling guilty for asking, was common for my sisters and I. I could see my mom's disappointment in not getting things she wanted for herself (she never asked for much). That said, dad worked very hard to provide a stable life for our family of five. In spite of the limitations our family experienced, I believed I could get whatever I wanted. I found lots of creative ways to make money.

I started working at 14 and saved enough to buy a car when I turned 16. Two years later I sold it for $500 more than I had paid. Can you imagine how excited I was at 18 to find out how easily money could be made? And how there are gains that can't be counted in dollars – like the use of a car for two years? My father could hardly believe it. I wanted to show him that there were lots of ways to make money, unexpected ways. Although, I had a different perspective about money, I learned some valuable basics from him. For example, he taught me to buy only what I could afford. That made me good with money, always putting some in savings and never using a credit card.

When it came time to choose a career, my chronic and debilitating health issues led me to pursue something in health care. With my strong work ethic (also learned from my dad), I always supplemented my income with side gigs. So, I started teaching at post-secondary colleges, and at 22, I established my first business. I was making really good money and was on my way to realizing my dreams of being wealthy.

Then, a very charismatic man came into my life. I thought he was amazing. Quickly after we got married, the relationship turned emotionally abusive; he was extremely controlling. Choosing to get out of the relationship hit me hard financially. He took a lot of my savings to pay off his debt. I had saved up and bought a house – half of it went to him. I put him through university, and still he got half of my savings account.

With the little bit I had left, I bought an investment property and tried once more to be really smart with my money. Some investments performed well and I got back on my own two feet again. I was very proud of myself and my ability to make money.

Well, you know what they say about pride!

I started to focus on the idea of being a millionaire by the age of 30. That meant I needed to find an arena where I could earn big money and was willing to work my butt off to make it happen. I left teaching for the field of real estate investing sales. Within two and a half years, I was their top producer, and I made half a million dollars. By 30, I was a millionaire – and I was married again.

Having money taken from me through the first divorce affected my perception of money. Now, the more money I made, the more I wanted, and the more I spent. It seemed the more money I made, the greater my anxiety about it grew. I had become addicted to money and the lifestyle that went with it; and I was more miserable than I'd ever been in my life.

At some point, a deep depression hit me. I was no longer doing work I was passionate about, I was juggling work with 2 young children, and the pressure to continue making the money to carry on with this lifestyle was weighing on me. If it hadn't been for my children, I'm not sure I'd even be here today. My addiction had to be addressed.

Although it was very scary to quit my $100,000-plus job and start a business doing what I loved in health care for zero money, I knew that in my soul, this is what I needed to do to release my attachment to money. There were a couple of really hard years financially. I left my second husband too, so I was a single mom, paying all the bills, trying to make ends meet.

That was when something else really big happened.

The real estate investing company where I'd worked, selling investments, defrauded us, and then went bankrupt. My ex-husband and I lost almost $300,000. Once again, what I thought I had was taken away. With the divorce and the fraud, my net worth fell from $1 million plus to less than a quarter of a million dollars.

All of my friends and family to whom I had also sold investments, also lost money. You can imagine the weight on my shoulders. I felt ashamed. I felt guilty for making so much money off of these people I loved and cared about. And now they would be losing their money too. I felt deeply that I was an embarrassment; despite having bought and lost just like they had. It didn't make me feel any better about it.

With my new company in holistic health, although I was struggling financially to make ends meet, I got creative again. I rented out my basement to ensure I had enough income to pay my bills. I worked tirelessly, putting every dime of the company's money back into the community. I did this for 5 years.

I served unconditionally and I dug myself into a financial hole. I had not paid myself in 5 years and to be totally honest I was exhausted, and my health was struggling... again. My kids saw their overworked, tired mommy trying to keep it together, and financially I was stressed out. I could not keep going in the same direction, and as I pondered going back to work and closing the business, I had to get really serious about asking for help.

Mentors came to my rescue. My team pitched in; I knew things needed to change, but I could not put my finger on why I could not pay myself. Did I truly believe I was unworthy? I prayed as I often do, and asked why I felt the need to work so hard, to try so hard. I needed to understand why I could not seem to pay myself when I was having trouble making ends meet.

I had up to 18 people on my team and they all got paid...why could I not pay myself? I did not understand. Why could I not seem to manifest the financial abundance I once had for myself.

This was the answer I received:

DeeAnne, you have been carrying the burden of money loss for others from the investments you sold. You felt it was your doing, although you were not the one who defrauded others. You took responsibility and felt it was your duty to repay this energetically back to the universe. This holistic business was that repayment. However, the repayment is now complete.

Oh my goodness. Can you imagine receiving this epiphany?! It all made sense to me now! I had been holding the unconscious belief that I needed to "repent," and that I somehow needed to "repay" the money I had earned when doing real estate investing.

You see, the $500k I had earned in my real estate time, was being repaid unconsciously through helping others to heal and succeed. As I did some calculating, can you believe that in 5 years of my business, approximately $500k had been put back into the company and community. I was SO relieved!

My self worth HAD been impacted, because I unconsciously allowed it to. My worth was attached to money and success. Here is the thing, though. Money is money, worth is worth, and they are NOT the same thing! The worth I have is completely up to me! Nothing or nobody else can dictate MY WORTH! Do you hear that?

Nobody and nothing can dictate your worth... except you!

Energetically, I felt a responsibility to the world. As I moved through this epiphany, I began to learn that money was just the tool I use to get other things. It wasn't who I was. It didn't make me happy or successful. My self-worth was in no way related to money.

Having this new understanding, this feeling of completion, brought so many changes. I found a new way of being.

Imagine Cinderella, no stranger to hard work, marries the Prince, is living a good life, then gets thrown back to having nothing again. I believe Cinderella's self-respect would mean she'd work just as hard as before and find her way back to the castle. Going from having money to not having money, and again to having money then not having money, taught me to be really present and happy with what I have right now. Attachment to things, outcomes, and expectations will set you up for disappointment, frustration, and suffering.

Remove attachment and your life will transform!

For most of my life, I had a poor quality of life. First, I was sick, then working 24/7 to put money away, and always doing things for others and not for myself. I drank alcohol a lot to cope with the things happening in my life, and I was constantly searching for happiness and meaning outside of myself. I had to make a bigger change.

I slowed down, stopped working so much, made myself my primary focus, and allowed things to unfold.

Now, I start each day with my focus on me, how I am feeling, if there is anything I need. As my children or clients need attention, the focus switches to them for a while then I bring it back to myself to regroup. You have to be whole and well to truly and consistently help others, so you need to take care of yourself first.

Taking care of yourself first magically brings abundance.

Now, I'm living the most abundant life I've ever had, and the good stuff just keeps coming.

Each day, I set clear intentions and act towards that, and it seems that by showing up, the abundance keeps flowing to me. My life is financially abundant; however, I am not attached to it – it can come or go as it wants. The current situation helps me take better care of myself and my children. That allows me more energy to be able to advance my company, and to help more people within that organization, which in turn again generates more abundance.

It has this crazy trickle effect where one thing feeds into the other, and altogether it's absolutely magnificent. I am clearer on my values and priorities as I continue to find creative ways to make more money, so I can help myself and others more deeply.

Remember: money does not dictate your worth, you do.

In order to experience your worth, you must focus on yourself by reaching into your heart and soul. In doing so, you will begin to remove your attachments to all that is outside of you. It really is that simple... however, not always easy. Otherwise, everyone would do it, right?

You can choose this for yourself right now. I know that when you begin to choose you, your life becomes abundant. What do you choose?

As the visionary behind Your Holistic Earth, the first comprehensive holistic healthcare network in Canada, DeeAnne Riendeau is changing the world with inspirational tenacity and positive energy. Nominated for countless awards, DeeAnne is a popular speaker, international bestselling author, and radio host.

Profoundly affected by a near-death experience in an early life fraught with chronic illness, DeeAnne rebounded with drive and determination to develop empowering solutions. A diverse health care career and Health Administration degree gave DeeAnne the insight needed to catalyze her revolutionary idea: expanding wellness education and providing affordable access to effective and transformational holistic healthcare.

DeeAnne Riendeau | Phone: 1.800.795.1389
Email: deeanne@yourholisticearth.ca | YourHolisticEarth.ca

Surviving a Brain Aneurysm:
The Signs I Didn't Miss!

By Evelyn Serbout

"I know my body is telling me something! I don't like how I feel!
I want my life back!" These were the words I said to our family doctor,
pleading for more investigation.

So many unforgettable and life-changing moments in my life happened in 2015 and 2016. I will never forget how many changes those years brought to my life.

In 2015, Calgary's economy began to collapse. Almost every household in Calgary was affected, and sadly, my very close and loving family was not spared. By the end of that year, my daughter (in August), my husband (in October), and my eldest son (in November) had all lost their jobs.

As a converted Muslim, I am a strong believer and a positive person. While this was happening, I submitted our lives fully to Allah ('God' in English). I thought I was handling it all really well, but in the midst of trying to portray positivity, I was actually in denial. Deep inside, I felt broken and afraid. To add to my misery, I started to feel dizzy and light-headed, for months.

I was thinking too much about my family, dealing with job loss. Our family's financial situation was at its worst! Even though we had all been gainfully employed and lived in a prominent area, we were still vulnerable. Without emergency funds, like many, we started paying utility bills, our mortgage, and even groceries by credit cards and a credit line.

For the first time in my life, I was experiencing STRESS! Not sleeping properly, I was lucky to get 3-4 hours of broken sleep per day. I woke up tired, with no energy. I lost all desire to exercise and felt the world's problems were all on me. My shoulders weren't strong enough to bear the burden.

June 2015: The Signal Event

In the summer of 2015, an ordeal landed me at the Foothills Hospital ER. That morning was a defining moment for me.

Muslims pray five times a day. In my experience, the more I followed the traditional Muslim spiritual practice, the more blessings I received. The first prayer, called *Fajr*, is performed at dawn. In the summertime, this means about 4:30am. During the first *ruku* (bowing), I collapsed, with no strength to control myself. My neck hit the corner of my closet. Thankfully, I didn't seem hurt, but when I tried to get up, I felt very dizzy.

In spite of what happened, I completed *Fajr* seated on my prayer mat. As soon as I was done, I crawled and climbed to sit on my bed. I tried to avoid waking my husband up – he had a busy day at work ahead.

Still sitting, propped up by a pillow on the bed, I closed my eyes, trying to sleep for a few more hours. No matter how I positioned myself, the dizziness didn't go away. After two hours, I started to panic. All kinds of negative thoughts came into my mind, including the memory of my Mom, who'd once had such a severe anxiety attack she almost died.

With that sad memory, a strong cold sweat came over me. I called the Health Line. When I told the person answering my call what had happened, she asked if I was with someone and said "Get someone to open the front door. I called 911 already. They are on their way. Hang up and get ready."

The fear going through my head was overwhelming – this was my first time going to the ER. That morning, the ER was busy. I sat, untended to in my wheelchair, until 11:00AM. When they finally came to look at me, the ER doctor said I had vertigo. He said, "You can go home, but I highly advise that you share what happened to you with your family doctor."

So that was it! My first ER visit ended just like that, with no other tests.

Mid July 2015: Seeking Answers

Two weeks later, my family doctor explained, "Evelyn, for someone to faint, get dizzy, or fall, it means the oxygen flow from the heart didn't go up high enough to reach the brain." He said he would send me to some specialists. I went home confused; still not knowing what was wrong with me.

The days and weeks that followed were very unsettling. The dizziness came randomly, every day. Sometimes long, sometimes short. I was in my lowest state of health ever.

I started searching for natural remedies. I was not offered any medical options, and I probably would have avoided them even if I had been prescribed something. My parents had many health issues, and their more severe symptoms stemmed from their medication regime. I lost them both due to complications caused by prescribed medications. My heart broken, I felt I learned a valuable lesson from their deaths.

I tried to find a way to resolve my symptoms by going to different natural product stores. I even bought some essential oils. Eventually, I was introduced to an all fruit and vegetable-based product line called **Triangle of Health.** Very impressed by the stories of health restoration that I had heard, to me, it was worth a try. I proceeded cautiously. I took the Triangle of Health supplement bottles to my family doctor.

I asked my doctor to check if the person promoting the products was telling the truth – the products had no pharmaceutical content. He confirmed it didn't. Relieved, I started taking the products. I quickly felt positive effects from the Triangle of Health. The products, easy to take, became my best buddy and I carried them everywhere with me. Feeling better was a great result. But my body was signaling that something deep within me was still unwell.

May 2016: Explanation — Aneurysm

Over 11 months, I did all the tests my doctor recommended; random dizziness and light-headedness still present. I felt really strange. I didn't like myself. I was afraid of falling again. Heart tests, ear test, eye test; all came back negative. My doctor said, "You should be happy, Evelyn." But he could tell from the look on my face I wasn't convinced.

> With conviction I said, "I know my body is telling me something! I don't like how I feel! I just want my life back!"

He asked, "What do you want me to do?" Persisting because I KNEW something was not right, I asked, "What other tests can you send me to?" He sat down, looked at his computer and after a few seconds, he said, "Maybe a head scan but, I will tell you right now (trying to avoid giving false hope), it might be awhile before you get a call. Your condition is <u>not an emergency</u>."

I said, "It's OK. It'll give me peace of mind knowing we're not stopping here." I truly believe God was on my side; in less than a month, the head scan was scheduled. Three days after the head scan, my doctor asked me to come to his office immediately.

I remember the look on my doctor's face when he said, "Sit down, Evelyn." Holding the result of my head scan, he started with, "They saw white matter in your brain." I was listening very closely, but my heart was beating rapidly, reacting strongly inside with, "I don't want to hear it." At the same time, I thought, "Hurry up! Just say it!"

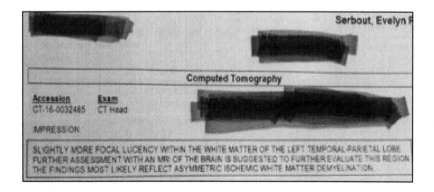

59

He said, "They think it's one of five possibilities: a brain tumor, a cyst, or early signs of Multiple Sclerosis, Dementia, or possibly Alzheimers."

Heat and numbness instantly engulfed me. All I was able to do was push back in my chair. In a shaky, crying voice, I said, "And you told me I should be happy. Now, it's not just one, but five possibilities!"

"The report highly recommends an MRI," he said. "I will make sure you get an appointment right away." Just 5 minutes later, he gave me the details.

I don't remember leaving the clinic. Next thing I knew, I found myself inside the car. I cried and cried and cried some more. So many fears and questions entered my mind, I sobbed like a child for a long time. I felt sad, broken, devastated. I eventually got tired of crying. I calmed myself by taking many deep breaths. A powerful verse in the Holy Quran surfaced: *God will not give you any burden you cannot handle.*

I told myself, "Have faith, Evelyn. At least it's not cancer. It could be worse." I drove home strategizing how I would share the news with my family without scaring them. Feeling strongly that God was with me, I managed to share the result with a brave face, with a calm voice, while hiding my fears.

Just three days after the MRI, the result came. My doctor again requested that I go see him in his office immediately. Why do doctors keep doing this to their patients, when they know it can cause anxiety and nervousness? This time, I brought my husband with me. While he held my hand tightly, the doctor said, "It was none of those possibilities that I told you."

I breathed a sigh of relief, but he immediately continued with, "However, the report shows a balloon in your vein. It's called brain aneurysm." My jaw dropped to the floor! In an instant, all the people I knew who'd died of a brain aneurysm flashed before my eyes.

All I managed to utter was, "How?" He explained, "Brain aneurysm comes from various factors; stress being the common culprit, and also lifestyle and age. But it could also be genetic. From now on, I don't want you to be alone. Have someone with you anywhere you go. Don't drive alone, don't even sleep alone. This balloon could pop even in your sleep. I will connect you to a neurosurgeon right away."

At last, the episodes of dizziness and light-headedness came to clarity: they were direct results of stress, not vertigo. I was so grateful they got it right this time. My husband made sure I was calm. As we went to our car, I silently repeated, *"La ilaha illa Allah"* ("There is no other god but the one God").

I was referred to a well-respected neurosurgeon named Dr. Sutherland. He explained I had two options; Coiling or Surgery. I instantly dismissed the coiling option – it wasn't complicated but required multiple follow ups. Knowing myself, I'd be more worried. I didn't need the stress!

I opted for brain surgery, in complete submission to God's plan for me. Dr. Sutherland required me to sign a waiver confirming my understanding that **I could die during surgery.**

August 2016: Preparing For My New Life

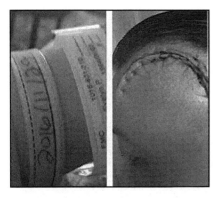

Another MRI, this time with injected dye, helped pinpoint exactly where the balloon in my brain was lurking. The surgery date: Tuesday, November 15. On the day of the surgery, it got rescheduled for two weeks. I thought I was supposed to avoid stress!

Surgery looming, love overflowed from family and friends. Five of my siblings drove 14 hrs, staying 7 days to show their support, just before the first surgery date. Beloved family friends, Mohamed and Aicha from Morocco, came as well and stayed for 14 days. Knowing now what I didn't know then, I realized that taking the Triangle of Health products were helping to boost my immune system and manage my stress response.

The morning of November 29th, I felt ready. *"La ilaha illa Allah"* were my fighting words. My husband gave me a kiss as the nurse pushed the bed to the operating room.

I closed my eyes and solemnly, I prayed. The words that came into my mind are between me and God. All I can share with you here today is that I am now living my prayers.

November 2017: My Call To Action

It took over a year for the numbness in my head to disappear. Dr. Sutherland warned me, "Evelyn, though externally it appears to be all well, inside it may not be. So please avoid getting your head hit or bumped, avoid slipping or falling." I promised to do my best, as I always do.

In the four years since the surgery, I've never felt dizzy or light-headed. Not only was I given a second chance in life, I feel blessed to be bringing my childhood dream into reality as well.

I have always longed to serve.

Keeping my promise made amidst my health scare, I continued giving back to my community through my school supplies program. When I eventually lost my job, I needed to continue supporting myself. I cannot afford the financial stress. I feel blessed by joining Kyani, the producer of Triangle of Health. I earn the same, sometimes even more, money as I'd earned in my corporate job. My husband loves his new job, and I am doing what I dreamed of. Able to support myself and my family, I'm ready for the future.

January 2020: Serving My Community

After three successful years giving school supplies to poor children on my own, my Outreach Program became a registered non-profit organization called **Outreach Program Canada.** Joined by the most wonderful people, we can now do a lot more for the community, locally and internationally. Our "*Give a Little, Help a Lot*" campaign allowed us to make almost 400 sandwiches for the homeless at the Calgary Drop-In & Rehab Centre.

Before the end of 2020, school supplies and basic necessities will be delivered to 365 school children in remote areas in Morocco. I am planning to do the delivery with a team of volunteers.

I am so proud and excited to see what's in store ahead. This is my dream come true, a true blessing from God Almighty.

I continue taking the Triangle of Health. I got more involved in the charitable programs of Kyani when I was appointed the "Wellness Ambassador for Caring Hands in Western Canada." Spearheading various campaigns in the last three years, I receive regular invitations to share my story with hundreds of people about my healing journey, in hopes of saving lives, one at a time.

April 2020: Now We Are Here

I learned my own important life-saving LESSON, and now I am living my LIFE. Sharing my journey, I hope, will make a difference for you.

An Important Learning: Don't be afraid to question your doctor's perspective. There is nothing wrong with doing that. For doctors, it means you are on top of your health. My doctor was appreciative. I like to say that a doctor has a body of knowledge, but you have the knowledge of your body.

My prescription: take care of yourself because You are important!

Our Divine Creator sends clear signs to you for a reason. Each of God's creations has a purpose in our healing. Some ways to care for you:

Love yourself. Give back to your community when you have the opportunity. By giving back and paying forward, you give love to yourself first. You don't need a lot of money to give, just Open Your Heart! Help whenever you can.

Feed yourself right. You are what you eat. Health is wealth. Often, we take our health for granted. Don't wait until you start feeling aches and pains; by then it could be too late.

Educate yourself. Learn your options. Consider incorporating natural products for healthier results. Medications can save lives, but they also have serious side effects. Perhaps your search will bring you answers you could never expect.

Support yourself. I learned that it is of utmost importance to know your body, listen to your gut feeling, watch carefully for the signs, the little nudges that tell us we must keep trying to understand.

When on a quest, especially about your health, do everything in your power to find the remedy or the answers you need.

Evelyn Serbout

- Proud "retired at 55" employee of The City of Calgary
- Founder/CEO, Outreach Program Canada
- Certification in Project Management, Mount Royal University
- Certification in Human Resources, Bow Valley College
- Volunteer, Ambassador for Western Canada, Kyani Caring Hands
- Volunteer, National Director Vice President and MAL Liaison, Association of Administrative Professionals
- Recipient of 2020 International Women Best in Volunteer Award

Evelyn Serbout | Phone: 403-836-8594
Email: outreachprogramcanada@gmail.com OR evelynlastinghealth@gmail.com
Facebook.com/Outreach-Program-Canada-2282299782020276/

How the Emotion Code Changed My Life
By Jocelyn Pettitt

If you are blessed to experience a moment in your life where your mind suddenly realizes its infinite power, a deep realization, a sudden awareness of your innate strength within, you are likely already on your own path of awakening or ready to embark upon your own spiritual journey.

I am fortunate to have experienced that precise moment. From here, I can look back and recognize that all my experiences in life carried me to this point, as though I was being divinely guided to recognize my own power to heal from within.

This journey of self-discovery and realization was so powerful that it led me to change the direction of my life dramatically in a short period of time. Healing myself from within has given me the one thing I believe is the most powerful force of change – *HOPE*. Hope for a different future, hope for different experiences, and hope for leading a fulfilled life.

I long to share with you how that realization awoke my inner spirit for change, and how I chose to rewrite, to reboot, and to plant the seeds for an amazing new beginning.

My childhood was not that different from most children; neither perfect nor traumatic. I can remember two major emotional events in my life. My parents' divorce and my father's death. After those losses, I remember feeling adrift and searching for God. I found my faith at the age of 19 and felt guided once again. I was surrounded by a community of spiritual people. I owned my own business, car, and condo by the time I was 21 and felt largely that my life was pretty successful. I got married at the age of 25, relocated to a different country, away from my family, and found myself in a relationship that would help shape me into the woman I needed to become.

It was not perfect. No marriages are. However, I know now that every minute of it was necessary for my growth. All the challenges and struggles served a purpose. Eventually, those experiences were the catalyst for a path of healing. I was blessed with three beautiful children who taught me unconditional love and gave me a purpose in life that kept me focused.

Eventually, my young family and I moved back to Canada, where I found a job as a school librarian. During that time, I came across a documentary on the Emotion Code, called *E-motion*.

After watching it, I remember that precise moment when I made the conscious decision to take control of my life. The documentary helped me understand that happiness was not in the hands of anyone but me, and that my happiness was a conscious choice that I was in complete and utter control of.

The documentary explained the theory of energy healing and the power of emotions over our physical bodies. I had always been aware of the influence of our thoughts and how they can affect our mental wellbeing, yet I had never considered the effect emotions had on our physical health.

It gave me a new perspective on how I view my life experiences. I was beginning to make the connection between an emotional reaction and a direct physiological response. I was intrigued by this process, this new form of healing our body, mind, and spirit and I was ready to participate fully in my healing journey.

Throughout the process of releasing my own trapped emotions, I began to feel more grounded and secure and yet lighter at the same time. I felt as though a literal weight was being lifted off my shoulders. Releasing these negative energies, stored in my body, began yielding surprising results. I saw evidence that I was regaining my emotional and physical health.

The changes I experienced were extraordinary:

- Headaches I had endured for over 19 years began to diminish
- I no longer needed to take anti-inflammatory medication (previously at least three times per week)
- I felt I was growing spiritually
- I felt a strong desire to live a more positive life

I noticed a change in my old triggers. Situations that might previously have induced a negative reaction no longer disturbed my inner peace. I stopped worrying about things in my life that were not to my satisfaction and focused on being grateful for everything that was right.

I was promoted in my job, and I became certified as an Emotion Code and Body Code practitioner through Discover Healing. This gave me the opportunity to share this amazing healing modality with others, and to feel a purpose in life that I yearned for.

Through my own experience of healing, and observing hundreds of my clients, I have come to consider the possibility that as much as 90% of physical pain or illness may have a root cause in trapped emotional energies within the body.

This is not a scientifically proven fact; however, through what I have witnessed in my energy healing practice, astounding improvements or complete recovery from pain, migraines, and illnesses occur once emotional healing is addressed.

Stress is known to be a contributing factor in health decline for many individuals. The Emotion Code modality offers a route to explore beneath the surface of a person's experience as part of their healing journey.

The following is a short description of the Emotion Code method, created by Dr. Bradley Nelson.

The Emotion Code is a healing modality that uses muscle testing to discover, identify, and release trapped emotions from the body. The method is simple and the only skills that are required are muscle testing and faith in the process.

With a developed connection between oneself and your creator, we can tap into the subconscious mind to ask questions about our energetic and physical body. While our conscious mind deals with day-to-day living and functionality of our lives, the subconscious mind is a wealth of information, recording every moment of our existence.

The book, The Emotion Code, describes various methods for muscle testing, and with this valuable tool and the Emotion Code chart of emotions, it is a relatively simple matter to discover the trapped energies within your body.

Once those trapped emotional energies have been identified, they can be released with the highest vibrational healing energy that exists – love.

As I reflect on my life, every major event, and the paths I chose, led me to this healing modality. Difficult relationships and emotional pain all served their purpose. Without those experiences, I wouldn't have learned the lessons that pushed me to grow spiritually to another level.

I wouldn't have sought emotional healing and engaged in deep soul searching had I not endured pain or suffering in some capacity. Once I discovered my true self, capabilities, and worth, I discovered that I had the power to change my future.

With this knowledge, I could turn toxic situations or experiences into an opportunity for growth. I began to alter my reality and help others do the same, moving through life without attachment to outcome. I discovered my ability to enjoy every experience; living fully present in the moment, absolutely carefree.

I maneuvered through my days with immense faith that all outcomes were for my higher good, and that my experiences and challenges all served an important purpose.

My successful energy healing practice empowers my clients to begin their own emotional healing journey. Together, we release trapped emotions and blockages. I feel truly blessed to have found a passion that fulfills me and provides an empowering service.

My practice, *Edson Emotion Reset*, is named after the small town in which I reside. The first year of my business, I exclusively worked on clients doing distance energy healing. However, during my practicum, clients were experiencing similar results with distance sessions as in-person sessions. The benefit of distance energy healing is that it can reach clients anywhere in the world. As my business grew, local clients began seeking my services and asking for in-person sessions which I now offer for those seeking a more tangible experience. The testimonials I receive from my clients regarding emotional and physical improvement – no matter where they are located – is a major reward for me in my healing practice. I am deeply privileged to work with clients from across the globe.

I am grateful that Dr. Bradley Nelson shared this gift with the world through his book, *The Emotion Code*. I offer Emotion Code workshops to bring awareness and spread the message that healing is a gift from within that we all possess.

I have witnessed many seemingly "miraculous" recoveries following an Emotion Code or Body Code session. I would like to share a few of my clients' remarkable experiences that stand out. (Testimonials available on my business page.)

Trigeminal Neuralgia and the Bulge on the Face

One client was diagnosed with Trigeminal Neuralgia, a debilitating disease that causes excruciating and continuous pain with very little hope of improvement. I worked with this client several times, clearing the Heart Wall and removing trapped emotions that we found in the location of the neck pain.

This client also had (what looked like) a bulging vein on the right eye that caused continuous pain; a visible bump that grew more inflamed or enlarged during times of stress, causing increased pain.

The vein was observed to be permanently bulged for about eight years. Doing a Body Code session for another client, I came across a reference in the Body Code System that identified a facial bone that appeared to be in the exact location as this bulging vein; it was called the Lacrimal Bone.

The next time I worked on the client with Trigeminal Neuralgia, I placed my focus on specific bones in the face. I discovered through muscle testing that nine emotions needed to be released from the Lacrimal Bone, along with others from the Nasal Bone, Zygomatic Bones, Nasal Bones, Vomer Bone, and Hyphoid Bone.

What I found really interesting about the emotions and ages that were trapped in these fascial areas was that they were pulled primarily from two time periods in her life, where relationships had ended and caused great heartache and pain.

Releasing what I found through muscle testing, my client fell asleep shortly after, feeling exhausted (as is common after this kind of energy work). When she woke up from her short nap, the bulge was no longer visible. For the first time in eight years, it was flat like the surrounding areas. Astonished, she thanked me repeatedly. When I followed up regarding the bulge; it had not returned. The client stated that, on a scale from 1 to 10, where pain had ranged from 8 to 10, it now consistently reaches as high as level 2.

Stabbed In The Heart – A Dream

A client who resides in another country was referred to me for unexplainable pain. She had endured much trauma and suffered emotionally throughout her life, and even more so since the pain began a few years prior.

I say unexplainable, because after seeing several doctors and trying multiple modalities such as chiro, massage, psychotherapists, cryotherapy, and electroshock therapy; nothing seemed to resolve, lessen, or explain her ongoing pain. Her suffering was so intolerable that she was diagnosed with Complex Post Traumatic Stress Disorder, Severe Clinical Depression, and Psychosis. After one failed suicide attempt, she hit rock bottom. Some days seemed unbearable to her.

After the first Emotion Code & Body Code session, my client reported an instant and noticeable mood change. She had the urge to bake again, something she had been incapable of doing over the last few years. She told me that she started to feel at peace within. This kind of change can only be understood if you yourself have experienced an energetic shift.

After the second Body Code session, she experienced better mobility and began to walk and move more. Prior to these sessions, she'd been afraid of moving for fear of the pain and spent most of her time lying down. After the third and fourth sessions, her breathing improved. She told me she had a rib that would continuously pop out of place. She would feel relief after a chiro session, but it kept happening regularly.

After releasing trapped emotional energies from her 1st and 2nd rib, as well as from her clavicle bone, she never again experienced it "popping" out of place, and her breathing returned to normal.

However, she was also contending with unexplained pain in the right scapular area for the previous three years. My client told me about a vivid dream she had before the pain began. She dreamed she was stabbed in the heart – and believed she had seen herself die.

My instinct led me to check for offensive energies. Through muscle testing, the Body Code system pointed me to a saboteur energy (an energetic weapon) that was present in my client in the same location she was experiencing pain. I explained what this was to my client and released it energetically with intention.

It was an amazing discovery, as nothing had ever explained the pain my client was feeling. My perception was that the energetic weapon, a knife, explained why she was feeling the pain.

It is still unknown how that energetic weapon was placed in my client's energetic body – whether through her own subconscious mind, or from dark intentions from another person, this might be a plausible explanation for the pain, energetically speaking.

We also found and released emotional energies, from the age of 14, off the Thymus Gland. Energetic imbalance of the Thymus Gland (according to the Body Code System) is connected to shoulder discomfort. I asked my client if she could remember anything that happened at the age of 14 years old, and she told me she was 14 when her mother had been murdered.

After we cleared the emotions, my client's pain substantially reduced, and she began working once again. My client has done phenomenally well since then, and is grateful for her Emotion Code / Body Code sessions. She is also grateful to all the health professionals who contributed to her recovery, in her quest to regain her health and quality of life.

Body Code Session on Four-Year-Old with Eye Irritation

I was asked to conduct a Body Code session for a four-year-old girl who had suffered with recurring eye problems for a few weeks. The mother sent me a picture of her daughter's eyes, which were inflamed and clearly irritated. I asked my client the obvious question: had she tried an antihistamine? She said she had and that it was not working.

The mom, who is highly intuitive, suspected that it was related to a "new" cat allergy that had developed shortly after a traumatic experience during a recent hospital visit.

The information from the mom set me on the right path to discover what was going on with her daughter's eyes. I did a distance Body Code session and discovered both viral and bacterial pathogen energies through muscle testing – which I immediately released energetically. I then released an inflammation energy and other emotional energies related to stress.

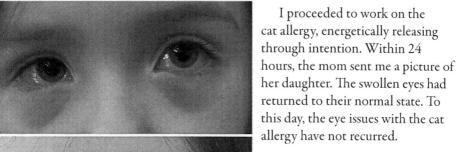
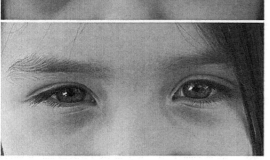

I proceeded to work on the cat allergy, energetically releasing through intention. Within 24 hours, the mom sent me a picture of her daughter. The swollen eyes had returned to their normal state. To this day, the eye issues with the cat allergy have not recurred.

I've witnessed many successful recoveries, ranging from cysts disappearing to unexplained stomach pains resolving to migraines subsiding; all following Body Code sessions. Many clients seek out this form of energy healing when nothing else seems to work for them.

The experience of receiving a Body Code or Emotion Code session is different for everyone. Some clients have a physical response: their pain is reduced or physical symptoms disappear. Others just feel happier, calmer, lighter, or more at peace.

I recognize that I do not have the qualifications to diagnose or treat any medical conditions, and I certainly cannot promise to cure anything for my clients. By sharing these client experiences, I am not trying to dismiss or discredit the work of other healing professionals. That is not my purpose.

My purpose, in sharing my healing journey, as well as a few client experiences, is to help bring awareness to the possibility that physical and mental pain may be improved by healing our emotional selves.

Healing ourselves emotionally causes a beautiful ripple effect that collectively raises the consciousness and vibration of the inhabitants of earth on a global level.

Expanding our thinking, while embracing the power we all have within to heal, is how *miracles* take place. The intention to heal allows the transformation to surface. It has become my purpose and privilege in life to share this gift in service to others.

The Emotion Code has given me the tools to lead my absolute best, most purposeful and graceful life. It freed me from emotional bondage and kick-started a level of personal growth and ambition that I once could have only dreamed of.

I am so honored to have the opportunity to inspire others through public speaking and client sessions. I am forever grateful to have discovered and engaged fully with my true purpose.

My prayer is that the people who need me, find me. That the Universe will guide whoever is ready to heal to what is best for them. I recognize the Emotion Code is one of many forms of energy healing. There are many beautiful modalities and lightworkers out there. This is simply my story of how I healed, and developed a skill that provided me with the means to give back to the world. The Emotion Code truly changed my life.

As a Certified Emotion Code & Body Code Practitioner, Jocelyn discovered her life's work helping clients release emotional baggage to live more fulfilling lives. A mother of three teenagers, she resides on a small acreage in Alberta, Canada. Jocelyn's distance energy healing practice allows her to work with clients across Canada, the United States, Mexico, Asia, and Europe. She also serves her community with in-person sessions. Jocelyn enjoys public speaking, teaching, and sharing her passion for empowered, authentic healing from within.

Jocelyn Pettitt | Email: edsonemotionreset@gmail.com
Facebook.com/Edsonemotionreset | Edsonemotionreset.com

Living A Life with No Regrets, Is A Life Worth Living

By Kehly MacDuff

"What happens to you does not matter. What you become through those experiences is all that is significant. This is the true meaning of life."
~ Unknown

Losing the person I loved most in this world, my mother Ronda Marie Hafner (1964-2005), put my life into perspective. The next life battle was one of my own. Not once but twice, I almost lost my life to a deadly disease called cholesteatoma. The loss of my mother, the suffering I experienced almost losing my own life, and the ways I have learned to thrive in the face of these challenges, has inspired me to share my story.

I grew up with a single parent, my mother. She battled depression and believed the world would be better off without her. She experienced profound trauma growing up and throughout her life, physically, mentally, and emotionally. The trauma was not only from this lifetime, but generational trauma that she took on as her own. The scientifically validated theory of Epigenetics indicates that pain is carried in our DNA, from generation to generation, until it is felt, healed, and forgiven within oneself and others.

As a young child (I believe I was about five years old), I witnessed my mother cut her wrist with a razor blade. She just did not want to live any longer with the weight of the world on her shoulders. An ambulance took my mother to the hospital, and she was admitted to the Psych Ward. My siblings and I were split up and put into foster care until my mother became stable enough to get us out of the system. She turned her life around within a couple months, and she wanted a second chance.

Once she won back custody of the four of us kids (I was about six by then), we moved to a new town. My mother worked her way through welding school and soon found a good job to support herself and her four children.

I was about 11 years old when we moved back to our hometown, where my mother got a full-time job welding.

My mother was still missing something that she had always longed for, to love and be loved in return. She struggled with her own self acceptance and self love, so she looked for it externally. She loved big, with her whole being, and would give her power away, doing things that did not match up with her core values.

My mother attracted a man with a history of using drugs into her life. Within a year, I witnessed my mother go from what appeared to be the happiest she had ever been, to selling drugs and soon becoming an addict herself. She would do her best to hide it from us, but we couldn't exactly ignore the strange people coming to our house at all hours of the day and night.

She told us: "If we want a good Christmas, and to have food on the table, I need to do this." Well that particular Christmas, my mother was nowhere to be found. She left us at home alone, with no food or gifts, on Christmas Day.

She began disappearing without a word to us for weeks at a time. Her battle with addiction started with cocaine, which led to crack, then heroin, within five years. We were removed from my mother's care again, and my siblings and I were sent to different places.

For long periods (the longest was 16 months), I did not hear from my mother. I would lie awake at night wondering if she was alive or overdosed in a back alley. Would she ever have the strength to get out alive?

Making many promises to get clean, my mother would try and get help, and I give her credit for her many failed attempts. I would beg and cry for her to get better and become the mom I knew she could be. I had little confidence in her, but I never gave up hope.

The morning of June 13, 2005, a day I will never forget, I received a phone call from my mother asking me for a ride to work. She said she was either going to die or go to work in the oil and gas industry as a laborer, stationed in a work camp for a month. She said she was going to try and get clean by herself. If she could leave town and the drug scene, she thought she could get clean and get her life back on track.

I was in grade 11, almost done with the school year. She had not been in my life physically since grade 6. I carried a lot of pain, hurt, anger, resent, abandonment, and neglect issues, just to name a few. I allowed those emotions to consume me. I was upset about being a little late for class, which was, of course, not the actual issue.

I gave her a ride anyways. She mentioned she had both a toothache and headache. I dropped her off at her destination without helping her with her bag, giving her a hug, a kiss, or an "I love you."

I had no idea this would be the last time I would see or speak to my mother. Battling an ongoing addiction, living a lifestyle that led to self-inflicted trauma and abuse, her life ended the next day, on June 14, 2005. A severe brain aneurysm had taken my mom.

She was my world. I was her cheerleader, and after her passing, I just wanted my mother back. What my mom would want for me, this poem puts perfectly into words:

"You can shed tears that she is gone, or you can smile because she has lived. You can turn your back on tomorrow and live yesterday, or you can be happy for tomorrow because of yesterday. You can cry and close your mind, be empty and turn your back, or you can do what she would want: smile, open your eyes, love and go on."
~ David Harkins

I learned from my mother's passing to cherish the people you love, always say "I love you," and never take any moment for granted, as it could be your last.

No One's "Listening"

I had a near-death experience, at the age of 24, caused by surgery, during an ongoing battle with Cholesteatoma. It started as a young child; over the years, chronic ear infections turned into this deadly disease, which ate away the bones in my ears, did nerve damage, and threatened my life. It took a long time for doctors to finally recognize the seriousness of my condition.

I had three major surgeries to rebuild and repair the damage, which I hoped would resolve my condition. Years went by, and I was still experiencing chronic ear infections. I was seen by many different doctors but felt as though no one was listening to me.

Physicians ignored my suggestion that the symptoms I was seeing them about were the same as my prior ear problems. I told various doctors I needed surgery to fix my condition, but they decided that surgical intervention was not necessary. They simply added to the stack of prescriptions they thought were adequate.

I finally refused all prescriptions because the medications and the doctors, too, were not addressing the problem. I knew in my heart that resolving this problem required another surgery.

I was fortunate to find a doctor who ultimately saved my life. Dr. Allan Ho was the first physician in five years who listened to me and agreed that my condition required surgical intervention. The night before surgery, I experienced the worst pain in my life. It felt as though my ear was about to explode. I knew I could withstand the pain until morning.

This particular surgery was scheduled to take four hours, but I was in the operating room for six. The disease had eaten a hole through my skull. The pain I was experiencing from pressure in my ear was from spinal fluid leaking directly into my ear canal. I was so lucky to have a doctor who was willing to listen; he ultimately saved my life.

Now I want to be the one to listen and heal with kind words, offer wisdom, and to give people an empathetic ear.

Have the Courage to Follow Your Heart & Intuition

My life experiences and challenges have empowered me to change. Growing up, I did not want the life my parents had chosen for themselves. I knew I had the power and strength to rise above the negative obstacles that were in the way of achieving success and happiness.

Knowing my parents were not happy about the choices they were making, I learned "life is about choices" and I wanted something different. My life offered two paths. The first was the route my parents took, which was unsatisfactory and unrewarding. The second was to pave a new way, one that would be a life worth living. I was fortunate to learn such a strong lesson at a young age, to realize that I had within me the power to change my life for the better. As an adolescent, the bad times were buffered by playing sports and trying to make healthy life choices.

Playing sports, I believe, saved me from going down the same path as my parents. My coaches and teammates gave me hope for something better than my reality at home. My passion for the game of volleyball, and my determination to be the best player, gave me the dedication to live a healthy, fulfilling lifestyle. That is when I learned: if you follow your passion and true heart's desires, miraculous things can happen.

Sports was a big part of my life; I always imagined the possibility of playing at an elite level. My hard work paid off when I was offered a full volleyball scholarship to Grande Prairie Regional College, where I played for two years. During that time, I accepted another full scholarship to play NCAA Division One Volleyball for the University of Arkansas at Little Rock.

My experiences with these teams taught me so much. I learned important life skills such as teamwork, organization, time management, integrity, respect, dedication, and perseverance, to name a few. In playing sports, I also learned how to stand on my own and work for what I was most passionate about.

Traveling is another passion for me; I have been fortunate to make this endeavor a reality as well. Over a two-year period (2012-2014), I travelled to Thailand, Indonesia, Philippines, Malaysia, Nepal, and India. I explored and studied different cultures, societies, religions, and lifestyles, but most importantly, I learned so much about myself.

Traveling to developing countries opened up my eyes and truly humbled me. The poverty, the people going hungry, the lack of education and resources. Witnessing how people with nothing to offer but their love and support managed to make it through one more day. The kids raising each other, while their parents went to work to try and provide enough shelter and food for the day.

I realized that my problems were truly first world problems. I had access to clean drinking water that came out of the tap. I had the opportunity to go to school and play sports, a foundation from which I was able to create a better life than the circumstances I was born into.

I discovered that happiness or love is not outside of us, it is within us. Once we are at peace within ourselves, nothing outside of us can sabotage it.

My life has been about dreams and working towards achieving what I set out to do. In following my passions, I set goals and work towards them. When things got tough, I would dig deeper and never give up.

Giving up is easy. Anyone can do that. But not everyone can keep working when the rest of the world would understand if you simply gave up. This was another lesson to be learned. Giving up is like giving your power away. If you believe in something, you possess the power to make it a reality.

Life's obstacles are never chosen. How we handle obstacles is a choice that defines the obstacle. I now see obstacles as opportunities that will help me grow and work towards becoming a better person.

I have learned to let go of preconceptions or old beliefs of what will or will not happen, knowing that anything is possible. Once I understood that the world is not black and white, and that rarely is it fair, I learned the power of releasing all self-blame and guilt towards myself and others.

Once you let go of trying to control the past, the miracle of life can be revealed in new and unexpected ways.

Empowerment comes when we can accept the support of others to assist in our life's journey. With my new-found strength, I want to share my ability to overcome seemingly insurmountable obstacles in life, that I never thought I could, with others who can use the kind of support and understanding that comes from walking a similar path. I've been there. I know what you are going through.

We all have the power to change our circumstances. We are not victims of life or society. The lessons I've learned on my journey have allowed me to inspire others to live a better life than what was planned for them.

"Happiness is not something ready-made. It comes from your own actions. There is no secret ingredient to happiness, it comes from within, and we all have the power to shine our bright light on the universe."
~ The Dalai Lama

I would love to support you, on your healing journey, incorporating a body, mind, and soul approach, as they are all inner-connected.

Services I Offer:

Strength Training Program

Online individualized strength and conditioning programs. I design high-quality routines that focus on the fundamentals required to excel in strength, power, endurance, mobility, stability, speed, agility, performance, and overall injury prevention.

Nutrition Clinician

The Diet Doc is your answer to failed cookie-cutter template-driven diet programs. Synergizing the science and support for enduring client success. Specializing in a macro-nutrient (protein, carbs & fat) based approach. Teaching clients the science behind nutrition and how to properly fuel their body according to their lifestyle, metabolism, and goals. Creating a lifestyle that is obtainable and maintainable.

Intuitive Energy Healer

As a Reiki Master, I assist in healing any emotional, physical, and energetic imbalances.

Kehly MacDuff is a transformational coach, healer/intuitive, strength and conditioning coach, and nutrition clinician. She played elite level sports, receiving a full-ride NCAA Division 1 Volleyball Scholarship from the University of Arkansas at Little Rock. She completed her Bachelors of Science Degree with an emphasis in Health & Exercise Science.

Her passion for sports evolved into a passion for assisting others on their personal journeys. She also loves to travel, and has studied healing wisdom from many traditions. Kehly empowers clients to heal emotional, physical, and energetic imbalances. Having overcome many of her own obstacles, she believes true healing encompasses a body, mind, and soul connection.

Kehly MacDuff | Email: Kehly@thedietdoc.com

Time To Change
By Lisa Wilson

The beginning of my story is not what I thought it was. I've realized, I had to look further back to truly understand. Normally, when I tell my healing story, I start with having half my thyroid removed unnecessarily, experiencing the biggest drop in my health. Five years later, I see that's not where the problem started.

In 2014, I was blessed to be laid off from a job at a company where I did not fit in. I say blessed because the three years I worked there were beyond challenging.

I knew my next step after that job was to start a coaching business. I'd kept working because I wanted to put enough money aside to ensure my ability to sustain myself, but I never quite believed I was ready. The lay-off seemed like the world giving me the kick I needed to follow my heart. Since it wasn't my own doing (terminated without cause), the company compensated me, providing me the nest egg I needed to get started.

Later that year, half of my thyroid was removed. It did not need to be. We still don't know what happened: might have been a typo on the ultrasound report, perhaps a growth that was healing itself. Either way, the lump was actually under the usual size of concern; which they aren't until they hit at least four centimetres, and they're usually slow growing.

Mine was biopsied twice and not cancerous, but they thought it had grown from 2.4 cm to 4.2 cm in six months. That IS unusual, so we decided to remove it. The doctor sat on his chair, elbows on his knees, head in his hands, fingers stretched across his forehead when he had to tell me that the lump they removed was only 2.4 cm. This was not good news; I now faced a life-altering outcome, no do-overs.

What followed was five years of tired. Not the type of tired where you can have a nap and feel better. A friend who has felt this calls it cellular tired. Tired to the core. Your body won't move. Your brain can't focus on anything more challenging than a Disney movie.

I spent days at a time lying on the couch, watching TV and movies that did not require any concentration. I couldn't work more than 3 days a week, and, if I exercised too much, even less.

I tried for a long time to get back to my "normal." My normal was cross fit, P90X, biking, cross-country skiing, working, volunteering, and showing up for everyone in my life. I tried many strategies but nothing worked.

I tried telling myself I was fine. I tried working out the way I used to. I tried changing my diet; but didn't stick to it because I craved the sugar that 'helped' keep me going. This treacherous cycle of sugar highs and lows can cause long-term damage, and I was already in trouble.

The low point was when I thought "I want to die."

I voiced to my boyfriend "I don't even like myself right now." It took almost five years to admit this, after countless fights with my boyfriend and step-kids who had moved in three years after the surgery. I had no patience for them. I'd become someone I didn't recognize.

Angry and resentful, I simply couldn't accept the "new normal." I was pre-diabetic. My doctor wanted to put me on cholesterol medication. I declined; I knew I could fix this particular situation without medication.

If you asked people who've known me a long time, they wouldn't believe this was me.

People still think I'm the most positive person they know, the strong and consistent one. No one would have predicted I'd get to such a low point. I didn't see it coming either.

Throughout my life and career, I've always been able to find a solution and move forward (or move on). I had endless energy and always found a way. Not this time. I could not see a way through this lack of energy, and I did not like who I was becoming.

I admitted to myself: this wasn't the first time I felt this way, just the first time it felt this deep. I'd felt this low before, but always depended on my energy to escape. Extreme exercise, a good vacation, adventure races, jumping out of airplanes, anything to boost my adrenaline and endorphins. I'd labeled myself an "adrenaline junkie." It was a joke, but I realized there's some truth to all jokes. I can see now that my "joke" was really acknowledging an addiction to exercise and being busy.

I was avoiding some serious issues; with no energy to make use of my 'fix,' my avoidance drug was no longer available to blow a smokescreen.

In my 20s, I was wise. My wisdom came from a willingness to learn, and an acceptance of what I was and was not prepared for. As I got a bit older, I made choices I came to regret, and arrived at a place in my life where I was so afraid to make a mistake, and so afraid to lose what I had built in my 9-5 job, that I misplaced that wisdom.

I decided, at 30 years old, that it was time to "settle down," buy the house, get the family, and know everything.

In my 20s and 30s, I worked for some great companies and some not so great. Fortunately, the good ones were first. I worked with a company that sent me on 6 months management training. When I turned down a management job at the second company, I felt comfortable enough to tell my boss I just turned down the job. She in turn told me what I needed to work on so that I didn't feel I ever had to turn another management job down.

I followed her guidance, and a year later, the job came open again. I became a Human Resources Manager at 28; my goal was age 30. This company was equally supportive and I spent three years learning and growing into my role.

My next goal? Buy a house. I paid down all my debt and put money into my retirement account to ensure I had enough to use for the down payment for my first home... that I purchased when I took a job in another city. Unfortunately, this and the next two jobs I had were not what I hoped, causing stress and behaviors I'm not proud of. The last job was the worst of them all.

They didn't present themselves honestly in the interview process, and simply put, I was not a good fit. I felt stuck because I lost money on the sale of the first home, and I'd stubbornly purchased a second home in my new town – against the advice of my financial advisor.

**Two months into the new role, I knew it wasn't for me,
but I stayed on for three years.**

Three years is a long time to constantly hear you are wrong. Even though I never believed them, my confidence took a big hit. Thinking back, I didn't like who I became then either.

Through these uncomfortable six years, I managed my stress by working out, taking coaching training, and starting my coaching business as a side hustle to the job I hated. I kept myself distracted by doing things I enjoyed.

I did a full round of P90X, 90 days of 90-minute intense workouts. I ran a half marathon (not something I thought I'd ever do) and starting doing Crossfit. The intense workouts kept me from falling deeper into those poor behaviours.

After my thyroid was removed, I didn't have the option to work out anymore. Five years later, I can still only do a 20-minute walk and 15 minutes of any kind of strenuous exercise.

**For a real change to occur, I apparently had to hit my rock bottom.
Everyone's rock bottom is different. Some actually begin planning their suicide.
For me, just thinking, "I want to die" was quite enough.**

I turned my mind to healing. It started with speaking the words "I'm depressed." This is hard to say when you think of yourself as the "strong one," especially when your doctor suggested it a year earlier, you'd insisted you weren't depressed... just really... tired.

I'd joined a mastermind with some amazing women. They heard me with no judgement. I also shared my feelings with my boyfriend and family.

I did things I already knew to get myself out of that despairing head space.

While I couldn't pursue the extreme exercising I'd used for too long as a smokescreen, I could walk and meditate every day. I made a major attitude adjustment: looking at my problems as mine, not the fault of the people around me.

Help soon started to show up for me. While my doctor found everything to be fine from a medical perspective, I knew something was off, and I decided to talk to a medical intuitive. She didn't tell me anything I didn't already know. I just needed someone to confirm my suspicions. I followed her suggestions and started to feel much better.

I started with a gut cleanse, and continued for several months on a candida diet. It was very restrictive, but I felt so good, I was able to keep it up this time. Bye bye, sugar!

During that time, I got to share my story on stage with the group of women in the Mastermind I had been in for the last nine months. It was the first time I got up on stage and threw away my script. I just shared my truth. It was unbelievably liberating. Since then, everything in my life seems to be falling into place.

I'd avoided Human Resources Consulting in my coaching business for some time, but I agreed to help a friend in her HR Department. I remembered that I am great at Human Resources. The negativity of that one job had alienated me, but no more. As I continued with HR Consulting, I was surprised that my struggling business was busier than ever.

While I share this as a challenging time in my life, I regret none of it. The jobs that didn't fit left me with wonderful friends. At each job, I made amazing connections – people who continue to cheer me one and support me in my goals.

I still struggled to write this chapter. The first line of my first draft was "I don't want to tell this story again." When I first shared it, I listed the following lessons:

- Listen to yourself.
- You don't need anyone to tell you what you already know.
- Let go of who you think you have to be.
- Take the first steps towards yourself and you will see how the world steps towards you.

While these ideas are helpful, as I move further away from the time of my life-altering surgery, and no longer live in fear, I see things differently now.

I learned that my problems began when I followed the "shoulds," comparing myself to other people in my life. Thoughts like:

- You should be married or at least be close to it at 30. All your friends are.

- You shouldn't go from owning a house to renting again. What will people think?

- You shouldn't share your truth; some things are meant to stay hidden. People might learn you aren't the strong person you've been trying to project.

Every time I let those thoughts win over what was in alignment in the moment, I got myself into a place where I felt "stuck." Decisions you make when you feel stuck are never the ones from the highest thinking part of your brain. Instead, those decisions come from a place of fight or flight. In that place, you can't see all the options in front of you. Seeing only limited options, none of the choices feel good.

More importantly, hiding out took me away from living my own beliefs and values.

I preach to clients "A leader's role is to model, teach, create, and develop a commitment to personal responsibility." I teach the importance of knowing and understanding who you are, grounding yourself in your Vision, Mission, and Values, whether working for yourself or leading at a larger company.

News flash: When you aren't living in alignment within your own beliefs, everything feels uncomfortable. It's hard to see what is causing all the stress. To shift out of limited perception, it's imperative to re-ground yourself in your own beliefs. I was running a coaching business and not practicing what I preached.

Consequently, my business was not where I hoped it would be. My situation felt hopeless. I had no idea how I was going to run a business, and worse, there was no way I could go back to a full time job. How could I, when I burned out in 3 days or less?

I had to accept that things weren't going to change. It was time to change me.

One of the toughest parts of my healing was thinking I could no longer be "the baker." I love to bake; doing a recipe I know well is a form of meditation for me. However, sugar and starchy carbs are not my friends.

It took a while to change my diet to one that supports my body, my adrenals, and my energy situation. I still don't always follow the new program properly, because it means changing how people know me and how I know myself. Shifting that takes work, but it's time to take care of me, now.

Slowly I'm moving from what tastes good in the moment to what makes me feel good long-term. My boyfriend jumped on board, making his own sauces and food without sugar, and we're actually enjoying all the new flavors, tastes and textures.

I can still be "the baker." I just need to use different ingredients.

This shift in my own life taught me so much and it has made me a better coach. I would stress when I could see the wisdom and need for a simple change in mindset for my client, but couldn't find a way to communicate it to them. I would wrack my brain between sessions trying to think of a way to help them see what I saw.

Now I recognize: we all come to our answers in our own time. I share what I see, and keep sharing until clients are able to hear it.

I've learned: Until we are ready, we won't hear it or make changes, and that's alright.

The side benefit of this newfound patience is that I'm now less judgmental than I used to be. I'm normal. There have been moments when I wasn't behaving in a way that I liked or that supported my health and growth, but I just choose and choose again.

We all have those moments. Be kind. Lighten up on yourselves.

Rather than beating ourselves up, giving ourselves a little grace and care will help us change our behavior much faster. Stressing about something causes more damage to our health than whatever that "something" is.

I'm sure there is more learning to come and more healing as well. I've come a long way, but I slip sometimes…

I overwhelm myself with work and volunteering, and that is when I go back to old habits. What's different now is, I see the pattern, forgive myself, say no or back out of something (even if I'm going to disappoint someone), and prioritize rest throughout my week.

I don't know if I'll ever be able to do Crossfit or P90X again, but now I focus on what I CAN do. I can still curl. I can still ski and mountain bike (just not as far).

I love the business I've built! It makes my heart sing when I work with a committed leader and help them see how their behaviour affects the team; helping them change what might seem an insignificant behavior; and witnessing the relief they and their team both feel when that small change makes a huge difference. The relief, happiness and confidence I see after working effectively with a client brings me so much joy.

When it's time to change, you will.

Healing (like any goal) happens over time, as you consistently implement and build on small changes. Setbacks are inevitable. I hope you decide to forgive yourself, and choose to do better again tomorrow.

When you open yourself up to new ideas, your healing journey will improve your life immensely.

Is it time for you to change?

Lisa Wilson is a Leadership Vision Coach and Human Resources Cultural consultant. Her passion is teaching medium and small business leaders to effectively lead their teams by creating exceptional workplace cultures. Witnessing the impact of both poor and great leadership, she now devotes herself to coaching leaders so their teams can experience the excellence they deserve. With 20 years of experience and training, she is set up to fast track you to become the leader you want to be. Lisa knows that great leaders can take their teams to amazing heights, and she invites you to find out how.

Lisa Wilson
Email: lmwcoaching@gmail.com | lmwcoaching.ca

Quarantine of the Mind: The Depression Dairies

By Dr. Louise Lightfoot

13th of February 2020

Here we are. The day before Valentine's Day and two days before the deadline for submitting this chapter. It is also the anniversary of my mum's death. Cheery. I am writing this awaiting a counselling session. It's not something I'm proud of. It hurts just to type it. I work in mental health. And that's embarrassing. Seeking help is the healthy thing to do. So I'm embarrassed. And I'm embarrassed to be embarrassed.

Perhaps this seems like a disappointing start to a chapter about health and well being. You could argue I'm doing myself out of job, as I am a psychologist. What a waste. I could be here selling myself or my strategies as the solution to all your problems. I might even refer you to my series of therapeutic children's books available now on Amazon... (Please buy and leave a good review.) I have to go in now. I'm being called.

15th of February 2020

Today was a write off. I did 23 steps according to my step counter. I'm secretly quite impressed with myself.

17th of February 2020

Question: *How can I help support people in their struggle when I'm so broken?*

Perhaps having mental health issues is a bonus for someone working in the mental health field. After all, the best person to buy a car from is a mechanic, right? Or a house from a builder?

Having mental health issues as a psychologist could arguably be a strength. It's authentic. You can support people with whom you can genuinely empathise with. I know I would rather be treated by a psychologist who had experienced poor mental health, so I can feel truly understood.

Unfortunately, you have to have good mental health to actually do therapy. I don't have good mental health right now. My editor has kindly given me an extension; I plan to write 3000 impactful and considered words as soon as I manage to get dressed (which I won't). I am treating myself with the kindness I deserve. Which right now is none. I keep threatening to go for a walk. Maybe tomorrow.

18th of February 2020

I got the idea from somewhere that becoming a psychologist would protect me. There is a genetic element to mental health conditions, which are prevalent in my family. I hoped knowing about mental health, the signs, incident rates, and strategies, might innoculate me against them and help me to combat my family history and the fallout of my distressing childhood.

Has that worked out for me? Not really. Turns out I know just enough to freak myself out, but apparently not enough to fix it. This seems to add to my shame, depression's trusty sidekick, making it so much harder to reach out for help.

I feel like I should have enough willpower and grit
to be able to will myself out of the hole I am in.
All hail Louise, she cured herself!

Well she didn't but she tried. Turns out, I'm not immunised and this virus is spreading throughout my system, unchecked.

My clinical knowledge is not the antidote. It just accelerates the intensity.

24th of Febuary 2020

I felt so bad, it took me several days to start writing again. I wish I didn't have to do anything at all. I have apologized all over the place for not getting this together, but I don't want to do anything. Even though I said I would.

It feels like *life* has its hooks into me and is trying to pull me back out of my isolated existence. I don't *want* to go outside and expose myself to more suffering, pain, and ooohhhhh, the VIRUS that is daily life.

Its drive irritates me, its action, its liveliness, its colour. Its determination to carry on. I feel like I'm living in the first half of Wizard of Oz. When Dorothy's farmhouse lands in Oz, all of a sudden things switch from black and white into colour; for me, my humble farm house is here, serving as a protective prison. I chose to isolate myself long ago. Well I didn't really CHOOSE. I had no option.

Inside this cell, nothing changes, and all I see is grey. I want to stay here. It's safer, quieter, and I find anything more than self-isolation to be too much to cope with.

The only thing worse than seeing only the grey is the guilt. Even though I am sort of safe in my isolation, it's hard to stay here: the guilt of doing nothing is crushing. Over a week in bed now, arguing with and beating myself up over my inability to get up, get better, get out into the world.

Knowing all the things that I need to do to feel better, and being unable to do them. I know connection, exercise, routine, and eating well will help. That's the work you have to do. I can't seem to do anything. I'm so overwhelmed by it all, and by life, that I just can't take part right now.

My previous accomplishments fade away. If we are the sum of our parts, and our parts aren't working, it's hard to feel like much of anything matters, let alone counts. A good friend told me once '*You are who you surround yourself with.*'

If you surround yourself with no one, it's frightening to realise how quickly you can come to feel like a no one. To feel like nothing. My friend is so right. But that is all I really want, because being me right now is hard.

27th of February 2020

Suffering with poor mental health is unpleasant. It sucks the joy out of you. You end up doing this depression dance... you go from not wanting to do anything to feeling bad about doing nothing back to not being able to do anything. It has ups and downs, ranging from uncomfortable but manageable feelings to paralysing and debilitating despair.

What compounds these feelings is the inevitable isolation that comes with the territory. The antidote, it turns out is... ta da... connection, not knowledge! Being depressed or anxious, that inner voice that tells us bad things isn't in the least concerned with what we know or with reality. It's about the way we feel or how our thoughts impact our feelings and behaviours.

It turns out the voice inside our head:
1. Has considerable power in terms of affecting mood and behaviour
2. Cannot be trusted
3. Can be fired/upgraded/altered, subject to effort and awareness

This 'internal monologue' often shoots Automatic Negative Thoughts (ANTs) at us, like bitey little ANTs that can be very difficult to ignore. We can come to believe these harsh little barbed zingers despite contradictory evidence. Letting them carry on unchallenged is how we lose sight of ourselves; we can slip into a deep depression or become crippled by anxiety.

I have promised myself (ok, negotiated with my internal monologue) that I would write for 20 minutes in order to earn myself an hour of nothingness. Seemed like a good deal. Time is up.

1st of March 2020

A famous British television presenter took her own life last week. After this tragedy, there was an outpouring of grief and discussion around mental health. The bromides and the fake concern nauseated me. The talking heads discussed how, as a society, we should protect mental health. How nice. They are the same ones who hounded her, knowing she was troubled.

For my own well-being, I've isolated from social media recently, but I had to write something about this tragedy on Facebook.

Caroline Flack was found dead in her home. Today there is and will be an outpouring of grief along with questions about how this could have happened. Well the answer is very easily come by. The easy thing to do is to post her picture and ask others to reach out if they feel that low. But that's the problem. Its like asking someone having an asthma attack to just breathe when what they actually need is an inhaler. When you are in the deepest depression and darkest of holes the hardest thing to do is reach out for help. The world just seems so far away and uncaring. I know this from experience. So I would urge to you spend the time you would have spent asking people to reach out to spend that time re-connecting with people you care about. Social media gives us a false sense of connection. It allows us to feel like we are keeping up with each others lives... auntie Karen is in Spain so she must be fine. Gina has taken her kids to the zoo so life must be good. We don't stop to think that maybe Karen has been bundled onto a plane as she hadn't left the house for 3 weeks. We don't think that trip to the zoo took everything Gina had and was motivated solely by the reason that the guilt she felt over being a bad mum was worse than her crippling anxiety. Everyone is so wrapped up in their own lives. And that's normal. It's inevitable. But that's alienating.
For those suffering it seems as if life is ticking over for everyone else while you can't even move. That's not to say people don't need to try to help themselves or to seek out support. It is important to acknowledge however that is an incredibly difficult thing to do in the midst of a mental health crisis. It's like asking a diabetic just to produce more insulin. You wouldn't expect that from someone who was physically sick so why do we expect more from those suffering mentally? The answer is we still think of the brain as being something we can control. We should we able to go for the walk, will ourselves out of bed, and eat more kale. But we can't. There are times when we are unable to do the things we need to do to make ourselves feel better. Even if we know what that looks like, especially if we know what that looks like. That adds to the shame. So instead of urging people in pain to reach out, try to reach in. I'm not saying that's easy, and it's hard to keep track of other people's mental health when most of us are just trying to make it through the day. But that's how it happens. That's how talented, good and most importantly loved people are lost. When you feel that low you can't remember who loves you, you can't remind yourself of what you have to offer the world. So sometimes those people need to be reminded. So look out for the people you love. Call them.

Has someone been quiet? Check in. They might not be ready to take a hand even if it's offered, but it's so important to offer it anyway. It's those offers, those connections, that pull you up to the surface. Sometimes you can't breathe on your own. You need an inhaler, you need a life line. So throw out as many as you can.

In my post, I challenged the recommendation, the GOOD ADVICE, that is so pervasive: ASK FOR HELP. SEEK SUPPORT. TELL SOMEONE.

As if it's up to the wounded to seek medical support. So many people urging others to 'reach out.' GREAT MESSAGE: the buck stops with **them**. The ones who suffer, in silence, feeling like the last thing they (we!) want to do is talk, or ask for help, or... do anything at all.

This post was shared and commented on more than anything I have ever put up on Facebook. People acknowledged how difficult it is to reach out for help when you are in the midst of despair or an actual mental health crisis. I got the sense that people who commented had experienced difficulties with their mental health. I knew that they knew I knew! Say THAT 10 times fast...

I have been hiding out, and pretending for too long. I have been in self-quarantine partly because my body has a tendency to betray me, but also because I just can't stand to try any more.

If you don't know what it feels like to feel so low that even suicide seems like too much effort, then consider yourself very lucky. The reality is that many of us have, are, and will experience intrusive and convincing thoughts encouraging self-destruction, and we feel truly unable to see a way out of the prison cell we have taken up residence in...

...because it's safer than the alternative. Until it isn't. That's why we lose people.

We believe the voice in our head that tells us that 'no one really cares anyway,' that we are a 'burden,' that everyone would be 'better off' if we weren't around.

If you listen to the nasty ANTs long enough, you can eventually convince yourself:

- You're doing the right thing, the only thing that makes sense.
- You're sparing the world of your noxious presence, the burden you impose.
- You're doing everyone a FAVOR.
- You're freeing up a cell for the next poor wretch.

It becomes the best and kindest thing you can do.

These thoughts cannot and should not be trusted. But they feel so real and seem to make so much sense.

2nd of March 2020

Bad news... I am way over my deadline. Good news... I've left the house and I'm back in counselling again. Reflecting on intrusive thoughts as I wait for my appointment to begin. There's a little questionnaire we fill in that tracks your mood. A question about suicidal thoughts, which, if you tick the box, you have to talk about it, asks terribly important questions like:

- Have you made a plan?
- Are these thoughts fleeting?

Problem. Big problem.

When you are genuinely feeling so low you want to kill yourself, really want to kill yourself, why would you tell anyone?

Surely the people who say and show they care would try and stop you, which is why suicide prevention shouldn't focus on the whys and how someone takes their life.

It's more important to understand how they got to that point. We need to start thinking of the brain as an organ like any other.

You wouldn't wait until someone was mid-heart attack to start looking at their heart health, telling them to just pump the blood faster, would you?

I want to know why we expect a similar capacity from the mentally ill?

A suicidal mind is not deterred by this. The end is what they think they want. They want the pain to stop, from a belief that nothing will ever get any better.

Cliche alert! Suicide is a permanent solution to a temporary problem.

We all know this intellectually, but sometimes our problems don't seem temporary, especially if you have become a Group 3 Dog. (See Group Dog experiment explanation, below.)

In other important news of the day, I washed my hair. I would really like some sort of medal.

4th of March 2020

So what do we do? We understand what makes our mental health better and worse, and then we do the work. I wish the answer was different but that is the unfortunate truth. This is the part that requires at least our complicity in terms of helping ourselves.

So what do we need to do? What does the work look like? Can we do this alone? The answer is we can't. We can do things ourselves to improve our mental health such as eating well, exercise, etc., but we cannot do it alone.

Loneliness and isolation are the enemies of wellbeing.

The impact of isolation on the human condition is so damaging that the UN have categorised any stay in solitary confinement longer than 15 days to be act of torture.

At the time of writing this I haven't been outside more than once in 18 days. Maybe it's time to leave the house.

Just my luck. There's a world-wide pandemic, and NO ONE should leave their houses now. Really???!!!

5th of March 2020

It's horrible being scared of your own brain, and of the thoughts it produces. As we have established, my internal monologue is an untrustworthy asshole. Was it ever nice? Is it like in the musical 'Wicked' when we discover that the witch wasn't always mean? The world made her that way!

Has the world made me this way, or can I change?

Well the good news is I wasn't born with these beliefs and feelings about myself and the world. I learned them, so I can un-learn them. But it's not easy. Our childhood experiences literally change not only our learned behaviour but also the very development of our brains. If we suffer in childhood, it's a lot harder to get healthy and well, and to stay healthy and well. So, no, it is not easy.

A psychologist might say I had a difficult life in terms of trauma. A psychologist might describe me as 'resilient.' I would have agreed I was resilient up until I was 30/31 years of age.

Before the end of Louise-as-I-knew-her, she'd done ok considering. Childhood felt ok at the time, she was loved. My mum was caring and gentle but suffered with severe mental health issues. She left when I was three, leaving me to be raised by my dad and older brother in a then-unusual male single parent household on a council estate in Liverpool.

I developed an admiration for my mum's perseverance as an adult, especially since I've had a taste of mental illness myself. I'm lucky in that my mental health issues are triggered by stressful events and are sporadic. My issue is that the issues don't go away.

Mum seemed to live with it constantly. From the outside my mum may not have looked strong. She was very placid and self conscious in person and worried terribly about just about everything. But she stuck around. People like her should not be perceived as 'weak' or 'broken' but as brave and determined.

7th of March 2020

OK. I have made you wait long enough, haven't I? The Dog Experiment. I'm sorry. I'm a psychologist. I have to tell this to you. Please bear with me.

91

Seligman & Maier conducted a series of experiments in the 1960's. Part 1 of this study consisted of three groups of dogs who were placed in harnesses. Group 1 Dogs were put in a harness and were released. Group 2 Dogs received electric shocks sporadically but they were able to stop the shocks by pressing a lever. Group 3 Dogs equally received shocks but its lever did not stop it. Group 3 Dogs learned that the shock ended randomly, and became inevitable and inescapable.

The same three groups of dogs were then tested in a chamber containing two rectangular compartments divided by a barrier which was a few inches high. All groups of dogs could escape shocks on one side of the box by jumping over the partition to safety. Groups 1 and 2 quickly learned to escape the shock.

The majority of the Group 3 Dogs however, who had learned that the shocks were inevitable, did not try to escape but merely lay down and whined when they were shocked. They literally gave in and accepted the pain. This inability to help oneself and succumb to undesirable an outcome was termed 'learned helplessness' (Seligman, 1960).

So the headline is if you perceive things to be out of your control, and you receive enough random and seemingly out of your control shocks, eventually you learn to give in and accept your fate, as painful as it might be.

Why is this relevant in this overdue, overlong article?

I'm currently a Group 3 Dog. If you read this and identify as a Group 3 Dog, that's ok. There's no shame in it. I hope this discussion gives you insight into why you feel such apathy. It made me feel better, like I wasn't just lazy. I think it's ok to fall apart.

I am a psychologist who is in the midst of a mental health... Episode? Crisis? Breakdown? Those words feel ironically action oriented. I do not feel like putting anything into action. It took me four hours to start typing. I have spent the last four hours arguing with myself. I'm exhausted. But at least now you know about the Dog Experiment.

Me and my inner monologue finally came to a compromise, I need to type for 15 minutes and reply to two emails. That's all I can take of life today, but it's an improvement.

I used to be a Group 2 Dog.

So what happened? Life. Life is what happened.

I was definitely Group 2 until I was 30. You might say, if you saw my true life biography, that I had lived through trauma. I was somehow able to power through it all. Until I couldn't.

It's horrible being scared of your own brain. And of the thoughts it produces.

9th of March 2020

I was determined to change my fate, to succeed in life, and I did. I got a scholarship to private school, went on to University and obtained an Undergraduate degree, a Masters, and a Doctorate, despite having dyslexia. I was resilient. I decided thereupon that I was an exception; I could work myself to achievement! Until, I couldn't. No fair!

I had three strokes in the final year of my doctorate program, and everything changed. My life was no longer in my control. I couldn't will myself to do better. I couldn't work myself into a better situation. I was literally disabled. What a mood killer. Or killer mood? Stuck in my body, in my home, and no way to escape. I definitely felt imprisoned. I lost all hope that I could manage, to ever make my own life.

It was a life sentence in a prison I depend on; no answers, no choice, no escape.

I took several more hits to my self-worth during the years following my strokes; the fallout included being unable to work, an industrial tribunal, losing my mum to cancer, and a general deterioration in my health.

The biggest blow: I was diagnosed with a rare, life-limiting, incurable genetic condition. This was a big difference from previous traumas, which had been episodic. This was like getting hit by a lorry. You just don't walk away unscathed. Your life will never be the same, and there is nothing you can do. My life felt out of my control, and I started to lie down. That's how I became a Group 3 Dog.

12th of March 2020

So what now? How do I get back up? Not easily, and not on my own. I can't will myself out of it; I have tried. What I have learnt is that no one has immunity to these struggles. No amount of knowledge can protect you from it. In fact, this might make it worse. No programme, no tablet, no remedy can get you through if you are trying to do this alone.

You have to be in the world and let it soak in. Obvious advice, but you have to start somewhere. It's small steps. Even though there is NOTHING I feel less inclined to engage in than the world out there. But I am a psychologist, so I will tell you what YOU can do. If you feel like it. If you want to.

Here, I have a few brilliant questions for you:
- What do you have control over?
- How can you plan your day to incorporate human interaction?

When it's time, and only then, reach out tentatively. That might mean replying to one text. Just one. Answer a call to a friend. Tell them, when you are well, what you might need when you are too unwell to care yourself.

Fight the shame. Talk to your postman. Help someone else.

Perhaps the most important thing to do is helping other people. I think that's critical to finding your way back.

Be ok with you, today.

It's ok to feel unworthy. Worthiness comes from seeing your value, and helping others is a great way to find that value.

In seeing how we all struggle, we see ourselves as human, as flawed, but striving.

You are more than the sum of your parts. You are enough. Success lies not in what you have achieved but in who you have become.

13th of March 2020

I have been writing my chapter as the rapid spread of the latest Corona virus is causing panic and fear. Isn't it ironic that I would almost finish this chapter focusing on the need for human contact and connection when currently such contact is now dangerous?

Despite its inherent difficulties, socialisation is key to staying well. And knowing we must refrain to save our own lives, well that seems to add to the frustration. The CDC guidelines state that any 'non-essential' contact should be avoided in preservation of our physical health. I have begun to wonder if we will finally start to view human contact as a survival essential? I want to call it an Essentialness. Is that even a word?

This stay-safe advice should of course be followed, but I wonder as to how this prolonged isolation will impact our mental health. We'll have to wait and find out, I guess. Is this a gigantic lab experiment? I hope that these extraordinary events teach us the value of human connection.

Arguably we have a pseudo sense of community as we feel like we are up to date with each others' lives due to social media, yet mental illness is at an all-time high.

We see only the highlights of everyone else's life, the polished, edited, and filtered version, and compare it to our reality. That gives our inner monologue all the ammunition we need to feel bad about ourselves.

So what's the answer???

We need to find a way to be kinder to ourselves. (I hate it when people say that.)

How? Tell me HOW, god damn it!

In truth, I don't know. No one does, I suspect. I haven't managed to fix mental illness despite my academic pursuits, experience, and god damn effort!

I am a microcosm. I am the problem and the solution. All I can do is reach for better feeling and thoughts. Put one foot in front of the other. And when I fall, and I will, make sure I have the best safety system available. Grab onto whoever or whatever pulls you up to the surface. Except I can't reach out and touch you. Not for real.

I don't think the world will be the same after this pandemic. People will surely hope things will go back normal. I don't. I hope not.

I want the people who are climbing the walls already after a week, complaining about isolation, to use that experience to appreciate how elderly, disabled, chronically and mentally ill people in our society live all the time.

What's upsetting people now is no one knows when things will get back to normal. When you are chronically ill, you know that date will never come. And the world isn't in it with you. So now MY life is 'normal.'

People with no familiarity with these restrictions are reacting without any sense of community spirit and activism. I hope it teaches us how fragile our mental health is; that we should nurture and protect it. I am going to try to help. To reach out. To share what I know and what I have learned. This crap ought to be worth something to someone else.

20th of March 2020

I am handing in my chapter today. It is a month late and needs editing. I've been so far down that the thought of completing this task felt insurmountable. So did eating and washing my hair. But I can see the surface. I am working my way back to the world.

I am determined to get back to being a Group 2 Dog.

How I would do it, if I could:
Be the change you want to see, show the love you want to feel.

PROLOGUE: Facing the Pandemic

I am getting better. Slowly but surely the grey state is passing. How do I know? When I first heard about the Coronavirus, I wasn't scared. I was indifferent. I thought to myself: "Bring on the flood." But the light is coming back on. The colors are fading in. It seems like maybe, I'm out of that cell, and now I'm hoarding toilet rolls at this moment...

Imagine that. A battle that I've survived.

It will all hopefully be over someday and I won't be in self-quarantine for my own reasons any more. Some people didn't make it due to isolation and loneliness before the pandemic. Many won't survive afterwards, unless we find a way to stay safely connected.

Oh. No. I must be socially responsible now, and stay home, to protect everyone ELSE. My days as a prisoner are not quite over, and I have no idea when this nightmare might end. No one does.

My days will be spent exactly the same. Isolation; but now, I have to stay away from others, in the service of society. At least I will have company. Come. Sit with me, but please keep your distance socially responsible.

Maybe we will share a cup of tea together. And talk about the weather, and wait for the sun to shine.

The sky... it looks beautiful. It's so BLUE.

As an Educational and Child Psychologist supporting 0-25 year olds, Louise champions at-risk or 'hard to reach' clients and communities. A triple stroke survivor due to Ehlers Danlos Syndrome (EDS) complications, while coping with life-long dyslexia and depression, she understands the challenges of living with learning/physical disability. Louise provides insight and expertise in mainstream/special schools, secure units, and psychiatric facilities. After winning a competition run by EDS UK, by writing a children's book about EDS, Louise developed an interactive book series, the first three focusing on mental health. She is committed to contributing to society, despite her circumstances.

Dr. Louise Lightfoot | Email: louise.lightfoot@hotmail.co.uk

From Rags to Riches —
My Financial Comeback

By Shanon Melnyk

The power was off more than it was on. The phone was disconnected more than it was connected. I grew up on a very humble farm, and by humble I mean poor. I can laugh now because the exact same pain I felt back then has now inspired me to WIN; the seven-figure kind of WIN!

I grew up wearing hand-me-down clothes, and not just from my siblings, as my brother was younger than me. Our farm neighbours were kind enough to leave us their children's clothes in one of my parents' vehicles; they did this to remain anonymous allowing us to keep some semblance of pride. I have never forgotten their kindness. It was like Christmas for me every time I rifled through to see what treasures I could wear to school. In those bequeathed clothes I felt like a beautiful little girl, rather than how I felt in my dirty, ratty jeans, cowboy shirts and boots.

We were raised around cattle and horses. We trained them, we broke them, and we showed them. I recall around the age of 12 (my brother was about 10), we each hauled 50 gallons of "chop" – a complex blend of grains, for the feeder calves before and after school each day. Back and forth we went from the feed shed to the corral, two five-gallon pails in each hand.

I learned a lot about cattle and horses but mostly about working hard; hard work that no child should ever have to do! I am very grateful because it taught me how to work hard to get results. I learned extraordinary patience working with those animals.

Every day after school, I would come home and watch Oprah. She truly inspired me because just like her, I too had a dream. I wanted to move millions of people. I still get emotional thinking about sitting there and feeling like I was made to impact other people's lives. I knew I wanted to do business even though I had no idea what that was. Have you ever had the experience where you didn't know what something meant or how to go about doing it, but just knew that was what you wanted? That was me. I had no idea how to go about being an entrepreneur; heck, I didn't even really know what that word meant. Watching Oprah so thoroughly inspired me that I wanted to be the "little white Oprah."

Although I loved our farm life because it provided us the illusion of freedom, I also learned a great lesson; in fact, it would become a huge part of who I am today and would shape my WHY to completely change my circumstances and myself. You see, at a very young age I realized that I had no interest in living a lifestyle where I had to work "that hard" to be "this poor."

Our house was in shambles; the front porch steps were often broken, the wood rotting to the point that we'd have to step over holes so we wouldn't fall through. The house certainly wasn't a priority and I understood that my parents didn't have the time or money to maintain a beautiful home. I suppose that has inspired me to keep a neat and tidy home today with absolutely no clutter. I am a minimalist.

Adding insult to injury, we had only very hard water which, being full of iron, turned all of our white or light-coloured clothes a beastly shade of orange. Consequently, my mom would drag her two ashamed children to North Battleford, Saskatchewan, the closest city at 30 minutes away, to do laundry at the local laundry mat. Everyone I knew had a washer and dryer in their home, but we didn't, we couldn't.

At 18, I moved to a bigger city, Saskatoon, to attend the University of Saskatchewan. There I believed I had found refuge. I couldn't have been more wrong. That experience was an epic fail and brought me great shame; after a year and a half of university, I got a letter from the Dean advising me to quit, otherwise I would be expelled. Of course, I took the "high road" and quit.

It wasn't all bad though – I met the love of my life that same year. Seven years later, when I was 25, we got married and had our perfect family – our beautiful boy and girl. Fast forward through 18 years of marriage totalling 25 years together, and I became another statistic. The inevitable divorce happened. I became aware that I had two conflicting thoughts: I had a victim mentality that was growing but also knew I was a very strong woman. This gave me the faith to know I could overcome this victim mentality, but how? I knew there had to be a better way to WIN.

After I quit university, I discovered the world of retail sales – this helped me realize that I didn't want to work evenings and weekends. So I did what I knew best – I went back to SIAST (Saskatchewan Institute of Applied Science and Technology) to become a computer programmer. I chose this path because it was the highest paying job at the time.

I worked in this profession for 10 years when I had a huge AH-HA moment that would be the start of major change for me. I had always heard that if you wanted to be rich, you needed to pursue your passion and work for yourself. THEN you will be rich. What passion to pursue? I was very passionate about photography. I was the high school photographer and I had been shooting my own kids' sports pics; I always had a camera in my hand. I guess I got that from my mom who is still very passionate about photography.

After completing a 10-year career as a computer programmer and then spending another 10 years doing photography, I knew there had to be a better way. I wanted to own my own business even though I had no idea how to run one. In fact, I had no idea where to even begin. I had heard that the goal was to earn income while I slept, but how was I going to achieve this? To top this professional soul-searching off, I was dealing with the fall-out from mental, verbal, not to mention sexual abuse. Gosh, I felt like, "When is my life just going to be easy?"

Soon, the answer came to me. When I was 38, my dad and Aunty Pat introduced me to the world of network marketing. At first, I absolutely refused to have anything to do with the profession. I had heard of these "pyramid schemes" and I told myself that they were for 'broke people that didn't have a life.' After six weeks of investigating, I realized I was "that broke person that didn't have a life" and I joined my first network marketing company. I was like everyone else – I didn't make money with my first company. It was the second network marketing company that would change EVERYTHING for me. I saw a VISION, hope in a bottle, and that product and that experience would be the start of change for me.

At 43-years-old I became a seven-figure earner in network marketing. I was, in fact, a MILLIONAIRE! It took me four years and less than an $8000 investment to earn my first million. That was life altering for me: this broke farm kid from small-town Saskatchewan had become a multi-million dollar earner in her ten-year career. Sure, I invested a lot of time and effort, but it was so worth it.

And then, all the victim memories, and so many more, came flooding back to create a massive 'victim story' within me. That story would take me on a life journey of more pain and self-discovery. I had never had money before in my life; I hadn't learned to deal with my money issues or my emotional and mental pain so I dealt with my childhood pain by "spending."

Have you ever heard of a BROKE MILLIONAIRE? Well, that was me. I travelled the world; I went to the UK 3 times, Singapore 3 times, Malaysia once, Australia 11 times, all over Canada, the USA, and Mexico. I bought beautiful, expensive purses and shoes. I rented absolutely stunning homes and condos. And of course I drove nice cars. It was a journey to heal, to heal me for my kids and for myself because I wanted to live the most beautiful, authentic life possible. In order to do that, I had to become a new person, I had to reinvent me. I knew I could keep doing what I was doing and getting the same results or I could change and get different results. The latter was the only option for me. I HAD TO CHANGE because the money wouldn't last.

The victim story that kept playing out in my head was, "Why me?" Through my healing journey, I learned that I had to be grateful for everything, everyone, and every experience. And so I did just that: I cried, I meditated, I journaled. I did so many things to be at peace with my past.

My biggest healing lesson was when I chose to forgive my parents and love them unconditionally. Our parents don't wake up every day and say "I can't wait to hurt my kids." Most humans wake up with the best intentions and they do the best with what they know. They honestly don't know a better way!

That decision was so healing! I think of Oprah and how she was raped daily by other family members and had a stillborn baby when she was 13. I think of Tony Robbins and how he had to fend for himself as a young boy and that his addicted mom tried to keep him sick at home just to have him with her.

When I get into my victim mode, I remind myself that my journey was my lesson and for that I'm forever grateful! It took a lot of work to heal and appreciate that my pain could have been much worse. I was truly so blessed!

In my network marketing career, I listened extensively to audiobooks and attended numerous courses by Bob Proctor, Tony Robbins, Jack Canfield, Abraham Hicks, Dr. Joe Dispenza and numerous other great teachers, all of which played a huge role in "me finding me." I was well on my way to working through my issues when I realized I had to deal with one more major hurdle. I had to deal with my MONEY BLOCKS. Why did money come to me so easily, but left me just as easily? I had no idea that my network marketing income would decrease exponentially over the next few years. I was spending all my savings to live "the lifestyle." I had to decrease my spending.

A dear friend kindly exposed me to the book "*The Illusion of Money*" by Kyle Cease and another dear friend challenged me to start doing *"The Magic"* by Rhonda Byrne. These two books changed everything for me. I discovered the world of "attraction marketing." I learned to appreciate money and be grateful. I was over low-ticket items, low commissions and my tribe not winning. I found a system, a funnel, a community, a culture, an educational platform.

Why is this important? I found a system that absolutely everyone can duplicate, from the strongest person in the tribe to the shyest person in the tribe. NO MORE NETWORK MARKETING FOR ME.

We live in a world where social media is our biggest asset as well as our biggest downfall. We need human connection. People need it and crave it, but it can be so hard to come by.

If you deeply care about people like you should, you should be having some conversations that actually matter. You can truly find out how you can help when you have the conversation. It could be about their relationships, etc.

It is the conversations and relationships that really matter. I eat, sleep, and build relationships. People are always trying to complicate how to build a relationship. It is so easy. Ask them about their family. Ask them about their hobbies, have the conversation, and get to know people.

I am just so passionate about changing and helping others by educating them about their options to win and be happy. I care enough to take the time and have a conversation and build relationships, heart-centred relationships.

I don't want to engage in the one minute fake conversation, I truly want to take the time to get to really know others. I crave deep conversations! I talk about the community, the educational platform, the personal branding, the digital marketing, and the automation because this is what people want in today's current environment. But don't ever underestimate the power in communication and building relationships.

It took me a life-journey to learn. It has really been the last three years that I have learned how to do this from a caring, loving, heart-centred place. One of the biggest gaps I see is not genuinely caring for people. That is one of the biggest hurdles people face.

People do business with people they know, like, and trust. When you care, you will succeed. You can't help but win when you truly care. Take the time to show people you truly care about them. Send handwritten notes or handwritten Christmas cards to all of your tribe. That is caring.

Be intuitive and find the right people. Not everyone wants what we have. As much as you think you want everyone in your tribe, that really isn't true. You have to decide and figure out who you want to work with. We are looking for soulful people who are really professionals at caring for others. The same $10 can do good things and that same $10 can do very bad things.

But money to me is beautiful; it's very important to us. It provides us with better experiences, it helps us provide our children with a better education, it helps us live healthier because we can afford better food and better choices. When we have more of it, we tend to live with less stress, which is highly beneficial because stress is the foundation of sickness.

When we teach others to earn more money, to budget more effectively, they tend to live healthier lifestyles and make better decisions, so they can, hopefully, donate to causes to help the less fortunate. It's important to give back and pay it forward because it's a gift to help others.

Today, I can say that I love my family, I love how I grew up, I wouldn't change one thing. I am forever grateful for the lessons and my own willingness to change and be better. I love money and money loves me. Life can be healing if you choose.

Remember, the first million is the hardest to earn. The lessons in life are priceless. The best way to win is to DECIDE... make the decision today! TOGETHER WE RISE!

An online marketer and branding coach, Shanon is crazy passionate about people. She was raised on a humble farm in rural Saskatchewan. She has one of those "get rich quick stories"...it took her 44 years to earn her first million with multiple millions of dollars in earning since.

A few short years later, she found herself budgeting and her pay checks crashing. Then Covid-19 hit and everything changed. While the rest of the world was wondering "Who ate the bat?" she was winning and changing lives! Her story is truly inspiring. NEVER GIVE UP, rags to riches to rags to... to be continued.

Shanon Melnyk | Phone: 306-220-3113 | Instagram: @ShanonMelnyk

Reshape the Relationship
with Business and Beyond
By Tricia Murray

There are some relationships we remember and others we don't. Some relationships change what we do, others transform who we are.

A decade ago, I would have believed I was more extroverted, but I have discovered that I am naturally more introverted, drawing power and strength from quiet. Even before I knew this, I would have chosen to hang out in a dog park over a networking function, and that remains the same.

I still love to travel and play golf; now I also kayak and meditate. I had learned about the premium prices that can be charged by making things complicated; today I delight in the value of simplifying and exploring depth. Today, I write, speak, and teach aspects of the work I used to do directly for myself.

I believe that it's possible to recover so completely – from the breakups, betrayals, and breakdowns – that we have to cause ourselves to remember the past. As I reshaped key relationships over the past 10+ years, standing across the bridge from a life lived 360° today, I have to make myself remember what life looked and felt like back then. Before.

My journey has been filled with research, study, experiential learning, and mentoring, and has distilled into a simple insight that holds a depth of power that can alter your life, as it did mine:

Humans are hard-wired for relationship.

We are innately wired to be social, which means we are naturally equipped with the ability to 'relate,' and we do. We *relate* to everything and everyone around us, and we do so through a 'relational lens.'

Why this base concept resonated with me so deeply, I don't really know... but it did. Perhaps it was a truth I needed to learn in order to experience more of life in every dimension. Perhaps it was a universal truth given to me so I could serve to enable others to create and experience more of their ultimate Endgame.

Regardless of 'the why,' my intention is to reflect, through my story, some of what reshaping key relationships, inside my business and beyond, has created and enabled me to experience.

The story of The Hunger Games™ became a metaphor, for me, of a dysfunctional and dystopian version of Business that creates an equally dysfunctional relationship between our work and every other aspect of our life – our health, people connections, spiritual enrichment, as well as time and money freedom.

In the movie trilogy based on Suzanne Collins book series, we see the extreme – antagonistic relationships created because of competition, conflict, and scarcity.

Twenty-four 'Tributes' enter the arena and there is an expectation and a very real need to compete, producing layers of conflict, as the most basic human needs are made scarce.

Until 2005, I had engaged in The Game of Business a lot like I engage in a game of bocce ball today; with a sense of light-heartedness, fun, and at times, pure delight.

But, woven into the fabric of North American culture is the inclination to take the innocence of a game – any game – into a gladiator pit of competition, conflict, and scarcity, to produce something that ends up looking and feeling a little (or a lot) like The Hunger Games™.

Two things shifted for me in 2005: First, my professional leader and mentor retired. She had been a strong, wise mentor and role model. Second, her replacement – a talented, skilled individual – was a seasoned veteran of The Game. She had played longer and more intensely than I had, since she had been playing where the competition was fiercest. Her relationship to The Game and the way she played it, inevitably influenced and changed mine.

I shifted from being able to identify when it was time to *make a change*, to resigning myself to *making it work*.

**Business and life can create a culture of competition,
but not everyone becomes a competitor.**

Relationships have the ability to inspire and infuse life into us; or they can drain the joy, passion, and sense of mutual meaning most of us want to experience.

My new leader brought in an entirely different set of expectations, objectives, and rules to play by. I soon found myself doing more, pushing myself further, and trying very hard to hold my ground. The new rules changed my relationship to The Game.

We were both on the same team; both focused on the same goals. Yet, we got locked into an antagonist relationship because we had entirely different Endgames in mind, which resulted in turf wars and competitive battles.

Relationships are built on trust.

I didn't trust her because the culture of competition and scarcity instills mistrust. Nor did I trust the Universe (or myself); I could not see that there was enough to go around, and that I could choose to do something new without losing the ground I'd worked so hard to gain.

My inner voice of wisdom (and circle of trusted friends and family) encouraged me to leave, while my rational mind (primarily the voice of fear) justified, coerced, and coaxed me into staying, repeating over and over: *"Better the devil you know than the one you don't."*

Point of fact: no version of the devil has ever proven 'better,' known or not.

Endless clashes between my head and my heart arose. I intellectually recognized that I was doing too much, pushing too hard; and I intuitively questioned if it was really worth the fight. That pervasive sense of scarcity overshadowed everything, as did my instinct to survive.

Each work battle left scars elsewhere in my life – on my personal relationships, my spiritual connection, my time freedom and eventually, my health.

She left, I stayed. My relationship with the work and business evolved. I took on more responsibility, became a co-owner in the business, which produced even more distortion around the role and purpose of the work (job, career, business). I knew something had to change, but quite honestly, I quietly hoped it wouldn't have to be me who initiated it.

I found myself in a holding pattern, waiting for something to shift. Hoping for something to change 'out there.' As I waited, the connection I had with the work, the business, and various other aspects of my life, continued to decline. I assembled a team of health practitioners to keep me upright. It was an initial consult with a naturopath that initiated a tectonic shift inside. She said,

"Tricia, there are things we can do together to support you, but until you are prepared to make more substantial changes to the approach you are taking to life, there is a limit to how effective our work can be."

Delivered with genuine care and kindness, her words landed at first like a feather, and then, years later, dropped like an anvil.

I was in a high-stress job, in a deadline-driven industry, running my domain of the business as a subset of a larger business. Her words landed like a feather because they didn't address my most immediate need: at that point, I felt like my body was betraying me and what I 'needed' were strategies to keep *making it all work*.

Continually 'making it all work' ultimately just makes everything 'work'.

Our *unconscious* mind knows when a relationship has run its course and when it's over. It tunes into the signs and 'messages' long before our conscious mind is ready to accept them.

The signs were all there. I just couldn't see them until someone connected the dots and reframed the relationship.

When I tuned into the deceptively simple truth that my relationship with Business wasn't working for me anymore, I began to reshape that relationship on multiple levels, a change that rippled across multiple dimensions. In doing so, I created more and experienced more – inside the business dimension and across a life 360°.

We've probably all heard the metaphor of displacement versus replacement. A glass of murky water clouded by dirt and sediment can be renewed in two ways; one is to pour the water out and replace it with brand new water; the other is to pour new water into the old, gradually displacing the original murky water.

Given that I couldn't "pour out" all that I'd learned after 30 years in business, or life for that matter, and that I couldn't simply dump out the stuff that didn't serve me overnight, it became apparent that displacing the old with the new was the only sustainable option, and it became the essence of reshaping, one degree at a time.

I *reframed* my relationship with my Body as I studied and practiced yoga and yoga therapy. I *realigned* the relationship with my Health as I worked with a variety of complementary and alternative medical practitioners. I *restored* a functional relationship with Work and Life, by stepping out of a dysfunctional one.

I reframed the relationship with my Mind; in my opinion, this is the intersection between our head and our heart.

I poured buckets and buckets of new water into my Mind as I realigned my worldview by studying everything from psychology to yoga to spiritual law and quantum physics over a seven-year period. I opened myself up to some of the most divergent thought-leaders of our time, and restored my resilience by mashing up what resonated for me.

I healed my relationship with my Spirit as I dutifully followed behind Ace, my Jatzu puppy, through every one of Calgary's dog parks, and I realigned from within through an expanding meditation practice.

I restored as I travelled and learned to paint, reconnected with people and met new, beautiful souls who became friends and mentors, teachers and guides. These loving companions reflected elements of a new relationship, for me, with business and beyond. Humans are hard-wired for relationship. We see EVERYTHING through a distinctly relational lens. We are also innately designed with the drive to create and experience more. Granted, not everyone leverages this 'drive' or works from the spirit in which it has been given, but it is there.

Looking back on my Business career, I saw how complicated business (and life) has been made, and why so many of us are experiencing less and less, as we do exponentially more.

Looking through my first and current Solopreneur endeavour, I have learned to embody more of the simplicity and depth of what is meant to be.

As my study of relationships moved in three directions – the business-customer connection; body-mind-spirit connection; and the connection between scientific and spiritual principles – each direction began to influence my business and the clients I strategically supported.

A theory emerged.

REFRAME

REALIGN

RESTORE

As we:

- *reframe* the role and purpose of Business,

And as we:

- *realign* key relationships in and around our business,

We can:

- *restore* our ability to create more and experience more through the business and beyond.

And there is a 'reflective' bonus: as we reframe, realign, and restore our own ability to create more and experience more, we enable others to do the same.

Abraham Maslow, a psychologist in the 1970s, framed a concept of our core, human needs. His 'Pyramid of Needs' (see image below) demonstrated that we are designed for more. Maslow and his peers discovered our innate drive to create more and experience more, as revealed through each tier of 'needs' in the Pyramid.

There is a time in our life and work (job, career, business) when we are solely focused on building a solid foundation. You cannot elevate your ability to experience more, if you are not working from a solid base – at work or in business – where your physiological and safety/security needs are consistently being met.

Abraham Maslow, Pyramid of Needs

Once the work has created a solid foundation, it becomes about something more.

The work (job, career, business) becomes more than a container that supplies our physiological and safety/security needs; it becomes a conduit for our belonging, esteem, and self-actualisation needs.

That reflective bonus shows up again: the work (job, career, business) is more than a container where *we* create and experience more personally; it becomes a conduit for us to enable others to do the same *through* our work, our job, our career, or our business.

During my reshaping process, I created more in intellectual capital and creativity than I had in the previous 20 years combined; meanwhile, I was experiencing more of life-giving rhythm in 360°. I was also having a blast doing it, with and for other people!

And then something shifted, again. It felt like I was slowing down, the way planets slow their orbit when they go retrograde. As I felt this shift, my relationship with 'relationships' went quantum.

The field of quantum physics studies the smallest elements of our universe; the tiniest little building blocks that ladder up to everything we see in the physical world. You may see a book or a tablet as you read this; quantum physicists see energy and matter, arranged differently – as a book or a tablet.

They learned something important about the behaviour of these tiny building blocks through the 'double-slit experiment,' which measured the path and the pattern of those tiny pieces, known as electrons. As each electron travelled toward a blank screen, physicists found that they 'behaved' in two distinct ways, depending on one variable.

The electron either created waves of impressions, like a pebble dropped into still water producing a corresponding ripple effect, OR it landed on the surface and created one impression, as if that same stone dropped onto mud or clay... no ripples, one single impression.

So, what changed? What was the ONE variable that turned the waves to a single impression?

The act of *observing* the electron changed its behaviour.

When I began to experience the shift; my relationship with creating and experiencing shifted as well. With the help of a unique mentor and teacher, here's what I found.

While I was still a "Tribute in The Hunger Games of Business," I got super-focused on one dimension – the work. I had masterfully manifested a <u>life</u> of work.

In the language of physics, I got laser focused on observing just one electron; one single impression.

As I worked through my own experience of *reframing, realigning, and restoring* the relationship, my focus was multi-dimensional. I was studying and travelling; connecting with new people and new ideas; traipsing around dog parks and interacting with yoga instructors that I loved. I start teaching yoga and eventually returned to the world of Business, supporting other Solopreneurs to reshape the relationship they had with their business (and beyond).

There was *unity* to my focus; this is what physics describes as *coherence* (clarity and consistency), but I was no longer focused on just one 'electron' (i.e., work).

I was focused on all of them (my health, people, work, time, money, spirituality) – fully engaged in creating and experiencing a life 360°.

In the quantum sense, spending time creating and experiencing multi-dimensionally, kept me in "wave function." The more I experienced in every part of my life, the more ripples I created.

But the minute I locked in on one electron, one dimension of my life, which for me, always defaulted to the work (job, career, business), I began to create less and experience less, because... no more waves, just a single impression.

It's easy to think of 'wave function' as 'being busy,' as we embrace the hustle or find ourselves to be pulled in 1,000 directions, which feels like chaos.

But the wave function can only exist in the presence of coherence. Without it, there are just a bunch of electrons flying around, with very few actually landing on the screen; and that, dear reader, IS chaos. That's when we start to feel like the struggle is very real.

If you'd like to explore more of the 'quantum' connection, visit:

www.becomingcoherent.com/the-quantum-connection

So, I have learned that it's ALL about the relationship:

... between our physical, emotional, and spiritual natures;

... between ourselves and other people, pets, things, and businesses;

... between us and the basic building blocks of our universe.

If you are not creating more or experiencing more, I'll wager a cup of coffee that something is out of alignment. When you are ready to try something different, 'more' can emerge by *reframing, realigning, or restoring* how you are relating to that 'something.'

We have a relationship with everything – our body, our people, our business, our calendar, the chair you're sitting in, and the quantum universe.

Reshaping the relationship with our business, our life, and beyond reconnects us with our ability to create and experience more through our business, our life, and beyond.

It's always about the relationship.

And here is the super-cool part: there is a reflective relationship between our world and the world we interact with.

As we unite the creation of 'more' with the experience of 'more' in our world, we enable everyone we interact with to do the same, because, as I learned and now teach: "There is no private good."
~Felicia Searcy

Tricia is a Solopreneur Strategist and Mentor to those who want to create and experience more, inside their business and beyond. Through a series of coherent, related pathways she facilitates and guides in reframing, realigning, and restoring their business within a life 360°.

Create more and experience more at
www.becomingcoherent.com

Tricia Murray | Phone: 403-461-6954 | Email: tricia@becomingcoherent.com
LinkedIn and Instagram: @becomingcoherent

Manufactured by Amazon.ca
Bolton, ON

12660694R00061